A CHURCH
TO BELIEVE IN

Peter C. Moore

Illustrations by Nancy Jackson

A Church To Believe In
Copyright © 1994 by Peter C. Moore
Illustrations by Nancy Jackson

First Edition, May 1994
Second Edition, August, 2000

Unless otherwise indicated, all Scripture quotations are
from the *Revised Standard Bible* © 1946, 1952, 1971,
1973 by the Division of Christian Education of the
National Council of the Church of Christ in the U.S.A.
Used by permission.

ISBN 1-893051-01-3

Printed in the United States of America

LATIMER PRESS
An imprint of:
Episcopalians United
P.O. Box 797425
Dallas, TX   75379
1-800-553-3645

For

J.I.P. and J.R.W.S.
meek men
mighty mentors

CONTENTS

Acknowledgements

As any writer knows, every book is to some extent a corporate effort. Not only have I relied on the ideas of many other authors in the production of this book, but I have asked several people to read early drafts and give me their comments. Special thanks goes to my stalwart editor Denyse O'Leary, who has helped me now with three books. I wish to thank the good people at Bristol House and Latimer Press, and in particular Jim Robb, who has given me many helpful comments. Les Fairfield, Paul Friesen, and Oliver O'Donovan offered their sharp theological minds to help me clarify several points, and to all of them my special thanks. Al Budzin helped me to see the manuscript through the eyes of a man with a deep Roman Catholic background. Nancy Ruth Jackson's illustrations and overall design have added immeasurably to its appearance and readability. Many people at Little Trinity Church encouraged me to turn what were originally lectures into chapters, and I also want to thank them for their continuing belief in my work. Last, though not at all least, I am grateful to Todd Wetzel for his counsel, vision, and support. Without him this book might not have been written.

Hoggs Hollow, 1993

Foreword

You will find this book is both a clear call for the Anglican Church to repent and also a means to bring us to a renewed understanding and appreciation of our comprehensiveness, which is an asset and not, as we often think, a liability.

Our Church is in a time of radical transition and transformation. It is thus a most appropriate time to revisit crucial issues that evolve around our ecclesiology. Here you will find a well-known evangelical priest giving serious thought to what God calls the Church to be as we move through a period of being re-formed and in many aspects of our life renewed or realigned.

Choosing five well-trained characteristic expressions of our church, characteristics that have often divided us rather than united us for God's mission, we are led on a fascinating examination of each one within a scriptural context. Using a most varied selection of historic figures to flesh out each of our different "parties," a clear picture of the diversity of our tradition is revealed. This is done not to diminish our differences but rather to point to the richness of our inheritance and to find that in such comprehensiveness may well lie our unity.

This book comes to us at a time in our history when our Church is fragmented and schism lurks close by, making this examination of the diversity of our tradition very important. For we do indeed need to find a new unity which emerges from our comprehensiveness. It is only too easy to see variety as divisive, while at the same time there is a crying out for the cessation of further fragmentation. By seeing the need in a whole and healthy Church to have all five characteristics, we are moved toward a much needed hope. For our Church does need to be

> Evangelical in experience
> Catholic in spirit
> Reformed in doctrine
> Charismatic in ministry
> Liberal in ethos
> Global in scope

In being so formed we are gifted by God and, as Anglicans, need to move toward the celebration in our Church of all its fullness.

We have often been narrow in our understanding and espousal of just one of these characteristics or perhaps even two! The Church needs to repent its past neglect of its wide, rich and comprehensive nature. The ingredients of that comprehensiveness need to be present in any Church which wants to express the fullness of its life in Christ.

It has been said of our Church that its watchword is "unity in essentials, diversity in non-essentials and charity in all things," a welcome reminder at this particular juncture in our life.

For if we are grounded in the truth of the gospel, we can serve the Lord of that gospel with our rich diversity and live together in charity. As the author points out, C.S. Lewis said it well, "Anglicanism deliberately seeks to concentrate its worship on the person of Christ, and its discipleship on obedience to the word of Christ." Our comprehensive make-up must be seen as a gift of God and as stewards of that gift our goal should be to use thus as a gift to offer to others that they may see the Christ.

It is good to have this examination of our nature — this refocusing of our task as we prepare for new days by doing things differently and in unity with God and one another.

Roger J. White
Bishop of Milwaukee

INTRODUCTION
Charting the course
— ❖ ————————————————

Like the contemporary map of Europe, historic
church boundaries are being redrawn almost as fast
as a cartographer can work. For example:
• A mid-size Pentecostal church in southern Georgia
is received en masse into the Episcopal Church amid
great pomp, circumstance, and ceremony — and an
outpouring of speaking in tongues.
• A professor of theology at Wheaton College weeps
for hours in his study as he resolves that he must
abandon Calvinism and become an Episcopalian. He
later writes *Evangelicals on the Canterbury Trail*, ex-
plaining why he and others that he interviews have
exchanged their roots in primitive revival churches
for Anglo-Catholic liturgy.
• Several staff workers of Campus Crusade for
Christ walk out of the organization they had served
for years, start churches, and then apply — as a
group — to become a part of the Antiochan Orthodox Church, a branch of Eastern Orthodoxy.
• At a meeting of the Prayer Book Society in
Toronto, I discover that one of the bishops in the
procession, wearing cope and mitre, is not a bishop

in the Anglican Church of Canada at all, but a former Anglican, now a member of a breakaway denomination called the Anglican Orthodox Church.

•Anglo-Catholic Graham Leonard, who grew up a conservative Evangelical and recently retired as Bishop of London, threatens to create a new denomination, free of liberalism and women priests.

•Thomas Howard, brother of Elizabeth Eliot, the famous missionary, and son to one of the great evangelical families of America, becomes an Episcopalian. Later he converts to Roman Catholicism, saying farewell to the evangelical tradition in a book entitled *Evangelical Is Not Enough*.[1]

WHAT SHOULD THE CHURCH TRY TO BE?

Such stories, which could be multiplied, illustrate the fact that as this century closes, orthodox Christians who have hitherto concentrated on piety, doctrine, and evangelism are now doing some serious thinking about the church. They are asking new questions, such as:

• What sort of ministry did Christ ordain?
• What kind of worship nourishes real faith?
• To what minimal standards of morality ought the church be committed in the public mind?
• How can we be free of excessive individualism in our piety and regain a sense of being part of the historic church?

• Where did the sixteenth century Reformation go wrong?

There is, of course, nothing new about these questions. Christians have been asking them for centuries. What is new, however, is that they are now being asked by Protestants who rarely glance over to the Catholic side of the fence, by Anglo-Catholics who rarely consider schism, and by Pentecostals who rarely appreciate liturgical worship.

A SEARCH FOR COMMUNITY, CONTINUITY, AND REFORM

At this point in history, there are good reasons why we must all think seriously about the church. First, the rootlessness of modern society has given many a hunger for rootedness. Os Guinness writes, "Severed from communal roots, the trajectory of American individualism has gone from the 'imperial self' of the unfettered and self-reliant nineteenth-century hero to the 'minimal' selves crowding therapeutic couches and recovery groups in the late twentieth century."[2] But the current quest to belong does not arise only from a desire for the warmth of home in the midst of the cold abstractions of modernity; it also arises from a desire by sincere believers to live their Christian lives with integrity. They desire depth and solidity, and this leads to a yearning for continuity with other Christians down the centuries. Their intellectual commitment leads to a desire to worship in a way that fully expresses their faith.

Secondly, the church is in trouble. When a prominent theologian says that the Anglican Communion is in danger of dissolution[3], when a leading bishop talks schism, when the American House of Bishops meeting in convention describes itself as "dysfunctional," when the newspapers report almost daily the sexual misconduct of some evangelist, bishop, priest, or monk, and when an ecclesiastical Court is summoned to legitimize a bishop's discipline of a priest[4], it is clear that the church is in trouble.

Thirdly, in addition to these troubles, there is the obvious fact that the mainline churches in Europe and North America have experienced a catastrophic decline both in numbers and influence. The church must be reformed, renewed, and revived. Robert Bellah, expressing doubt about whether such a renewal is likely, writes: "Unfortunately not only the Protestant tradition but the Catholic and Jewish traditions have undergone severe attrition in America and in their present form it is doubtful whether they can provide the basis for genuine cultural renewal."[5] But whether renewal is statistically likely or even culturally relevant, one thing is certain: it will not happen unless we have a clear idea of what the church should be in the first place.

A COMPREHENSIVE VISION

The six short chapters in this book are aimed at taking a fresh look at the church. Each focuses on one of the words that describes the church founded on Christ by the earliest Christians — or, at any rate, one of the words that *ought* to describe it. The first five words, I deeply believe, should be characteristic of every church: evangelical, catholic, reformed, charismatic, and liberal. While these terms are conventionally used to describe parties or wings within the churches, I hope to show that each rightly belongs to the whole church. None ought to be neglected.[6] When a party or a whole denomination neglects any one of these descriptives, it is seriously deficient. I make no apology for drawing many of my illustrations and references from the Anglican heritage which is my own both by birth and by choice. Furthermore, my last chapter testifies to my hope that the comprehensiveness which the Anglican church has always claimed for itself may one day become evident to others and an example to the wider church.

Each chapter includes a brief analysis of a passage from the New Testament which, when examined in the light of our questions about the church, shows why the descriptive word under discussion is appropriate. At the same time, I endeavor to show that when any one of the five words — evangelical, catholic, reformed, charismatic, and liberal — is adopted to the exclusion of the other four, the church becomes seriously deficient. I also aim to show how each of these words challenges us to be the church in all its fullness today.

MY HEROES OR YOURS

To flesh out the meaning of each word, I introduce my readers to an historical figure who, in my opinion, best exemplifies that strand of the church's life. Because they were Anglicans, they are part of my own heritage. Non-Anglicans will be able, I am sure, to point to similar heroes within their own traditions. I encourage them to do so. I have purposely chosen my heroes over a broad expanse of time. They come from the early sixteenth century through the twentieth century. I regret that only one is a woman, and yet I believe that the influence she wielded in her day may have been as wide as that of several of the others I have mentioned.

Part of my intention is to assist clergy and laity in the renewing of our minds about the church. Ecclesiology, the study of what the church is, was taken for granted by many people in former generations. It has become a burning question today as we see churches torn asunder by theological, ethical, liturgical, and social issues. "Be babes in evil; but in your thinking be mature" was Paul's advice to the Christians in Corinth because their naive views of the church were being challenged by the party spirit that erupted within the body there.[7] By thinking rightly about the church, we worship God with our minds as well as with our hearts, just as thinking about what Jesus Christ came to do in creating his church helps us to worship him in "spirit and truth."

The corporate nature of Christianity is part of our faith as confessed in the Apostles' and Nicene Creeds. Jesus did not come to create a conglomeration of individuals, each with a private belief system, preferred style of worship and personal piety. He came to create a peculiar or distinct people, who, like Israel of old, would be a light to the nations. To be the people he intended us to be, we must hear God speaking to us in new ways and challenging us to new faithfulness in our corporate life.

PILGRIMAGE

It was Karl Barth who spoke about our fundamental need for not one but three conversions. The first is to Christ, the second is to his church, and the third is to the world. For me, the second of these conversions was the most difficult, because my early experiences of the church were not such as to inspire either loyalty or interest. The church in which I was brought up, a suburban Episcopal congregation in an affluent community, had many creditable aspects, I am sure. However, for a young boy or teenager as I then was, it held little attraction. The sermons on *is-ness* and *was-ness* by the learned rector, though doubtless pregnant with deep theological meaning, became objects of ridicule around the family dining room table. Our understanding of the significance of these insights for living the Christian life was further obscured when he ran off with the church secretary and abandoned the Episcopal Church!

But the "Hound of Heaven" was not about to give up on me so easily. In time, the Grace of God found me out. Realizing that church attendance was an inherent part of my new commitment, I proceeded to experiment by attending the services of various denominations. Each of the Protestant churches I attended for a while had a certain appeal. I experienced community, fervent corporate prayer, evangelistic and expository preaching, rousing hymns, and an intense focus on missions. But when I was urged by some to be rebaptized, told by others to seek a particular experience of the Holy Spirit, or refused communion because my theology was incorrect, my enthusiasm began to wane.

I returned to the Anglican fold, which in my heart I had never really left, one Ash Wednesday evening after wandering into a lovely colonial church in New Haven, Connecticut, to attend communion.

A stranger to the community gathering that evening, and perhaps for that reason I paid particular attention to the words which the minister used in describing the non-litergical eucharist that evening. I heard nothing about the blood or broken body of Christ, nothing about sin and forgiveness, and nothing about death and resurrection. Instead, I heard that the loaf symbolized our unity as a people, the wine our shared pain and suffering, and that the act in which we were engaged was a corporate remembrance of the love which, enfolding us from our birth, was now uniting us. I silently made my way to the door, thankful for the knowledge that, however meaningful that act was to those who were there, there is more to holy communion than that.

My subsequent experience of Anglican congregations in three countries (England, the United States and Canada), and brief stints in Anglican churches in Europe, have given me a bird's eye view of the remarkable diversity that goes under the label "Anglican." Each of the five words with which I describe the church in the following chapters typifies one of the different congregations with which I, my wife, and growing family have been associated. While grateful for certain emphases in each congregation, I have been saddened by the striking ignorance — at times even hostility — which each of these strands has revealed towards the others.

FRAGMENTATION

Quite apart from the shameful superiority which Anglicans seemed to feel towards non-Anglicans (often expressed by veiled condescension), the inability to appreciate the contributions of other strands in the church revealed an intolerance that was not of Christ. Why was the Anglican Church engaged in dialogues on Christian unity with Methodists, Lutherans, and Roman Catholics when her own house was so fragmented? What could our church's incomparable liturgy, majestic architecture and rich hymnody offer to the wider church when she was racked by party spirit and mutual distrust? And what possible relevance did she have to a generation whose quest for spiritual reality was side-tracked by the subtle illusions of modernity — the credit card, the video store, and "safe" sex?

We need to listen to the Word of God again if we are not to be torn apart by issues arising from the women's movement, the sexual revolution, and inclusive language, and if we are to recover what it means for the church to be the body of Christ in which each member has vital functions to perform. On the subject of listening, William Willimon of Duke University, responding to a query about his hermeneutical approach, once said, "When I open my Bible, I recognize that this book knows more than I do, and so I say to myself, for the next twenty minutes it's going to ask the questions."

If the following chapters enable us, from whatever wing of the church we come or to whatever denomination we belong, to appreciate each other better, they will have served part of their purpose. But my long-range goal is more adventuresome.I pray, as do many, for nothing less than the recovery of that rich tapestry of truth and life which comes when the church listens to and is obedient to the fullness which God has revealed, and when she refuses to accept reductionist visions in place of true comprehensiveness.

ENDNOTES

1 Nashville, Nelson, 1984.

2 *The American Hour: A Time of Reckoning and the Once and Future Role of Faith* (New York: Macmillan Free Press, 1993) p. 305.

3 W.S.F. Pickering, *The Study of Anglicanism* (London: Fortress, 1988), p. 374. Many besides Pickering have raised this question!

4 1992, Diocese of Toronto.

5 Robert N. Bellah, *The Broken Covenant* (New York: Seabury Press, 1975), p. 109. Quoted in *The American Hour*, op cit., p.388.

6 F.D. Maurice (1805-72) in *The Kingdom of Christ* held that the particular vocation of the Church of England was to hold together various polarities which historically have spawned new denominations. See *The Study of Anglicanism*, Stephen Sykes and John Booty, eds. (London, SPCK, 1985) p. 37.

7 I Cor. 14:20.

He turned the city upside down

Charles Simeon was for fifty-four years (from 1783 to 1847) Rector of Holy Trinity Church in the heart of Cambridge University. He turned the city upside down with his clear, expositional sermons. Although they were first received with intense hostility, they eventually won over both town and gown. It has been said that no prelate had a greater influence in England than this peculiar man who was both dreaded as a dangerous enthusiast and praised as an evangelical statesman. How can this 19th century Anglican preacher, who loved and served God with all his heart, help us to understand the church today?

EVANGELICAL
The word of promise
and challenge

— ✣ ————————————————————————

CHARLES SIMEON may be one of the best known
19th century evangelicals. Almost immediately upon
his appointment as Rector of Holy Trinity, a storm
of controversy erupted, because it was known that
Simeon had fully embraced the evangelical witness
during his undergraduate days. With the full support
of his bishop and with his undeniably potent gifts,
Simeon brought an uncompromising spirit to his new
work. But because the late eighteenth century's attitude towards religion was generally one of comfortable skepticism and social convenience, any serious
Christian witness was viewed as "dangerous enthusiasm." Therefore, neither the town nor the Church
wanted what Simeon had to give.

The seat-holders (people who paid for their
pews) deserted the Church in a body, and locked
the doors of the pews, so that no one else could use
them. When Simeon placed benches in the aisles,
the wardens threw them out into the churchyard and
for more than 10 years those who came to services
had to stand. Outside the Church there were

tumults and uproars as people tried to prevent others from coming in. Inside, bands of undergraduates tried to break up services. Simeon was so despised that once, when another member of the university greeted him on the street, he went immediately to his rooms and wept.

But Simeon labored on at Holy Trinity for over half a century! Over time, through his loving persistence, a generation of evangelical clergy was raised up and trained by him to preach. Because of his special concern for foreign missions, he helped start the Church Missionary Society which sent scores of England's best to distant lands — not just as chaplains to British colonists, but to work with natives, something almost unheard of in that day. Simeon bought the right to appoint clergy to parishes, a common practice in England, thus ensuring an evangelical succession in those parishes to this day. Always loyal to his bishop and to the Prayer Book, Simeon's messages were sincere, powerful expositions which invariably pointed to Christ.

Gradually he won over the hearts of the people. In later life, when he preached at the University, no faculty member who could possibly be present was absent. When Simeon died, the whole university shut down, the town closed, and thousands lined the streets to bid him farewell. Simeon's enduring legacy is the continued strength of evangelical witness in

Cambridge University and through the world-wide Inter-Varsity movement which began there.[1]

REVIVE THY CHURCH

Simeon would have insisted that all talk about the church must begin with Jesus Christ as Lord. He created the church. He purchased it with his blood. He animates it with his Spirit. The church exists only as it is united to him by faith, as it draws its life from him in love, and as it seeks to be faithful to him in obedience.[2] Without the living Christ, the church is simply one of the many institutions in society that can be understood sociologically. But with the living Christ, the church becomes part of our faith, the "one, holy, catholic and apostolic church." With the living Christ, the church becomes a mystery visible to the eyes of faith.

But Simeon would have insisted that faith must bring us back to the individual. Christ builds his church one stone at a time, one person at a time. This is not individualism. It is merely a realization of the critical importance of each Christian having a lively personal faith. Any Christianity that ends with the individual simply ends. But unless Christianity begins with the individual, it doesn't even begin. Or, to switch metaphors, the church is Christ's body on earth. It is like a human body in that most of its cells must be individually alive or else the body is headed for the grave. Of course, again like a human body, the church contains a number of dead cells. But these must be at the periphery of the body, for example, surface skin, hair or nails. If the majority of a body's cells are dead or dying, life will not continue. And while cells do frequently try to survive on their own, in mutiny against the body which nourishes them, they become either parasites or cancer cells, and the whole body suffers — often fatally.[3]

When we recognize that individual faith is essential to the life of the church, we are reminded of why the word "evangelical" is crucial for any understanding of the church. A church is evangelical when, within its fellowship, all that Christ has done is made immediate and personal to us as individuals. It is of little use to say that Christ loves the church, calls the church, and is united to the church if people do not sense that he loves, calls, and is united to them personally. Until each knows that Christ loves, calls, and is joined to them by faith, these are just words.

DISPELLING THE CARICATURES

Two churchwardens from a church on the other side of the city from my parish were telling a layman from my parish about their struggle with decaying buildings, dwindling numbers, and declining revenues. They were fascinated by our parish's apparent signs of health. They quizzed him about our stewardship program, our newcomers committee, our youth ministries and so on. They seemed willing to try anything to get their parish back on track — until our man mentioned evangelism. Evangelism? Their faces paled, nervous coughs followed, and the conversation seemed to move quickly on to other subjects.

There are many reasons why people are frightened by the word "evangelism." Howard Hanchey writes:

> Evangelism is associated — at least in the minds of many...with emotional fervor, intellectual bankruptcy, partisan politics, and naivete. Others, more favorably inclined toward the term, are tempted to confuse it with renewal movements, the need to increase church membership, or even the visitation of new members.[4]

Authentic evangelism is the proclamation of Jesus Christ in such a way that individuals are confronted with a call to repentance and faith. Where it is part of the ongoing life of a congregation one finds people who are individually discovering the new life which Christ promised. No church that fails to evangelize can be called evangelical!

WHAT DOES IT MEAN TO BE *EVANGELICAL*?

To be evangelical, a church needs more than evangelism. At the heart of a truly evangelical church there is, above all, a receptivity to the Word of God. There, by the power of the Holy Spirit, people hear the Word of God not only as a given, as revelation "once for all delivered unto the saints,"[5] but also as a personal message inviting response. People discover a community attuned to the message of a God who speaks, whose gift to his people — as at Pentecost — is the ability to hear through the words of witnesses precisely what God wants them to hear.[6]

> Therefore, brethren, since we have confidence to enter the sanctuary by the blood of Jesus, by the new and living way which he opened for us through the curtain, that is, through his flesh, and since we have a great high priest over the house of God, let us draw near with a true heart in full assurance of faith, with our hearts sprinkled clean from an evil conscience and our bodies washed with pure water. Let us hold fast the confession of our hope without wavering, for he who promised is faithful; and let us consider how to stir up one another to love and good works, not neglecting to meet together, as is the habit of some, but encouraging one another, and all the more as you see the Day drawing near.[7]

PROCLAIMING THE UNIQUENESS OF CHRIST

First, the church must be evangelical because the uniqueness of Christ is central to its confession. For over ten chapters the writer of this epistle has extolled the utter superiority of Christ and his total adequacy as God's agent of revelation. Greater than the prophets, Moses, the angels, and greater than the entire priestly system of the Old Covenant, Jesus in a unique and final way had reflected the glory of God by bearing in his person the very stamp of the divine nature.[8] To the writer, the response to this is plain. Given this once-for-all revelation of Christ, the church must "hold fast the confession of its hope without wavering."[9]

The evangel which must be at the center of the church's witness is not primarily a subjective experience — not even a subjective experience of faith, if by that one means that the gospel's focus is on an internal psychological event. The interiority of faith is subsequent to and utterly dependent upon that exterior witness to the uniqueness of Christ which we find in the apostolic writings. Whenever the church fails to take seriously its task of holding on to the biblical insistence that in Jesus Christ God has been revealed in a final and decisive way, it falls prey to various trends which, while seeking to give Jesus a prominent place in the scheme of things, deny him the preeminent place.

However, the Christian is not to cling to this past witness the way a drowning person clings to a piece of dead wood. Hebrews stresses the graceful nature of this news, which reveals a second important feature of a church worthy of the name evangelical — its ability to see God's revelation as good news.

GOOD NEWS, NOT GOOD ADVICE

The form in which the Old Testament came down to us was as law and promise. The law stressed the holiness of God, and called for our obedience in response. The promises of God, enshrined in both the prophetic books and the wisdom books, stressed the faithfulness of God and called for our trust in response. While this is to some extent an oversimplification, it helps us to see that, while Jesus fulfilled both the law and the promises (as well as the wisdom) of the Old Testament revelation, those who claim to follow him have not always kept these elements of our faith in proper relationship to each other. Legalists, both biblical and modern, focus on the law and tend to receive the Word of God primarily as bad news rather than as good news. Since the law holds up a standard of behavior which is impossible for mortals and sinners, legalists must disguise their own bad consciences underneath a cloak of rectitude. Akin to legalism is moralism, which appears to soften legalism and rescue it from its terminal pessimism by seeing the Word as "good advice". But moralism is really only a variant of legalism, because it too neglects the other half of the Old Testament witness, the promises of God.

In Hebrews, while the moral demands of the law are upheld for New Testament believers[10], the primary focus is on the faithfulness of God, who has fulfilled his marvelous promises to his people. It is because the young church saw in God's faithfulness his loving consistency to his Word that they were led to live lives of faithful integrity often at great personal cost, as Hebrews spells out in graphic detail.[11]

The contrast between legalism's forbidding face and the evangelical focus on the faithfulness of God is made throughout the book of Hebrews. In Chapter Twelve, a passage rich in symbolism, New Testament worship is compared with Old Testament worship. While the latter is distant, gloomy, ceremonious, slightly fearful and full of guilt, says the writer, the former is alive, festive, forward-looking, reverent, and full of thankfulness.

THE CENTRALITY OF THE CROSS

A third feature of the church found in this passage is its joy in the experience of a clear conscience. The writer relates this joy directly to the blood of Christ, linking his death to the sacrificial rituals of the temple where an animal's blood was sprinkled on the altar to signify cleansing from sin. Because of the blood of Christ, that is, because of his life outpoured in death for us, we can go straight into the presence of God. This amazing thought, which surely must have astounded the writer himself, means that the deep yearning within the human heart for reconciliation with God can be fulfilled because of what Jesus did on the cross. There is no need to fear rejection, because the curtain has parted and a new and living way into his presence is now opened for us. Guilt over past wrongdoing can be put behind, and as our bodies were washed in baptism, our consciences are now cleansed through the cross. No person needs to tremble any longer before the holy God. The great priest, the ascended Jesus, is standing at God's side on our behalf. Surely, to every believer this is marvelous news.

Søren Kierkegaard came to a new realization at Easter in 1848 that God had not only forgiven his sins, but "forgotten" them. So he wrote a moving sermon on Luke 7:37, the passage about the woman with the alabaster jar of ointment whom Jesus forgave.

> The Christian who lives many centuries after Christ, when he is tempted by the doubt whether his sins are forgiven him, will find comfort in hearing as it were Christ saying to him, "Believe it, nevertheless, for I have laid down my life to procure the forgiveness of thy sins; so believe it then, a stronger assurance is impossible." ... Only when Christ is offered as the sacrifice of atonement ... is the comfort at hand which makes the doubt of the forgiveness of sins as impossible — yes, as impossible as it possibly can be.[12]

An insistence on the centrality of the cross is always a distinctive mark of an evangelical church. Just as the evangel celebrates the once-for-allness of God's revelation in Christ, it also celebrates the once-for-allness of God's redeeming act on the cross.[13] In the words of a famous old hymn:

> *There was no other good enough*
> *to pay the price of sin;*
> *He only could unlock the gate*
> *of heaven and let us in.*
> *O dearly, dearly has he loved!*
> *And we must love him too,*
> *And trust in his redeeming blood,*
> *And try his works to do.*

From the discovery that the Gospel is truly good news flows the church's missionary impulse. As news is for sharing, evangelism is inherent in the nature of the evangel. Since the New Testament word for "preach" literally means to "herald the Gospel", the Christian is like the gaggle of lepers running back to the city to announce (amazingly) that the enemy has fled, leaving everything behind, as the prophet had foretold — so everyone is reprieved.[14]

BLESSED ASSURANCE

Fourthly, the church is evangelical because believers can be assured of their salvation. The writer of Hebrews communicates a striking confidence that the work of Christ is sufficient for our future salvation. We may come to God with "confidence," have hearts full of the "assurance of faith," and we need not waver because "he who has promised is faithful."

The Christian doctrine of assurance is an evangelical distinctive that rightly belongs to the whole church. When as a young Anglican priest John Wesley encountered a group of Moravians, they impressed him with their sense of assurance. Noticing their lack of fear of death in the midst of a storm at sea, Wesley approached their leader, who asked him, "My brother ... does the Spirit of God bear witness with your spirit, that you are a child of God?" "I was surprised, and knew not how to answer ... I know he is the Saviour of the world ... I hope he has died to save me," said Wesley. "But do you know yourself?" asked the Moravian. This question troubled Wesley until several weeks later, hearing an exposition of Luther's commentary on Romans at a Moravian Bible study in a house in Aldersgate, Wesley's "heart was strangely warmed" and he wrote:

> I felt I did trust in Christ, Christ alone, for salvation; and an assurance was given me, that he had taken away my sins, even mine, and saved me from the law of sin and death. [15]

Sadly, many in the church think assurance of salvation is presumptuous because they have never grasped, or been grasped by, grace. They still inhabit

31

the realm of law, and expect salvation to be granted them on the basis of their good works.[16] But as St. Paul wrote to the Romans, peace with God is not a vague aspiration. Rather, it is the confident assurance that we are right with God, on the merits of Christ. We are not saved by our own goodness, nor even by some dramatic spiritual experience — as Wesley has sometimes been misinterpreted as implying — but solely on the basis of Christ's atoning sacrifice for us.[17]

Donald Bloesch, who rightly roots our assurance in the promises of God, warns of the dangerous tendency of revivalism to locate the ground of assurance in a crisis experience of conversion. He reminds us that Jonathan Edwards, who rooted our assurance in God's fidelity, nevertheless linked our ongoing awareness of that assurance with continued obedience. Edwards said: "Seeking and serving God with the utmost diligence is the way to have assurance, and to have it maintained."[18] This, doubtless, is also the corrective needed for those who feel only a minimal sense of sin and fall into the opposite trap of thinking that salvation is, of course, assured — like Social Security!

The sacraments are given in part to remind us of the assurance that we have by faith, and to strengthen us in that assurance. When Martin Luther felt himself under spiritual attack, he would remind himself, "I am a baptized man." Similarly, in the Holy Communion service in the Prayer Book, the "Comfortable Words"[19] are potent reminders that our assurance of salvation is based on the sure promises of God in Scripture, not on our own feelings, one way or the other.

REDEFINING OUR VOCATION

Fifthly, the church must be evangelical because there is a job for every believer to do. Hebrews puts it this way: " ... let us consider how to stir up one another to love and good works, not neglecting to meet together, as is the habit of some, but encouraging each other." This early church pattern of lay ministry was rediscovered by the sixteenth century reformers as the doctrine of the "priesthood of all believers." Over against the priesthood of the priesthood, they taught that every Christian has a vocation before God.

However, it was two hundred years before this Reformation insight into the New Testament began to be translated into the everyday life of believers, except among Anabaptists, who vigorously asserted this doctrine in the 16th century. While the church's theology was right, its structures still reflected the medieval focus on the clergy. The Catholic priest had simply been replaced by the Protestant presbyter. But during the evangelical revivals of the eighteenth century, the wind of the Spirit blew through Europe and North America, leading believers to discover ministry as something to which all are called together. It was this discovery which helped bring to the church a sense of true fellowship grounded on the concept that all are "brethren" and are called to love one another and to demonstrate their faith by their good works.[20]

The following, then, are the essential emphases which the word "evangelical" guarantees for the whole church. While they are drawn out of the passage in Hebrews which I have highlighted and, as I have suggested, they are strongly underlined elsewhere in this remarkable epistle, they are found throughout the New Testament, and should be the bedrock of every congregation's experience:

- Jesus Christ as the unique and sufficient revelation of God, brooking no rivals, inviting no comparisons
- the Word of God as a personal message to us as individuals
- the death of Christ as central to our message, offering us clean consciences before a holy God, and inviting us to pass through the veil into direct communion with the Father
- the message of the Gospel as good news which replaces legalism and moralism, and impels us to proclaim, to everyone who will hear, God's faithfulness to his promises

- the whole people of God as priests, each with a vocation to minister as God leads
- the church as a fellowship, where love is made concrete in relationships and in good works.[21]

DANGERS FROM SYMPATHIZERS
AND FROM OPPONENTS

When separated from other aspects of the church's life, these emphases can create churches which are individualistic, separated from history, overly personal and chummy, and consumed by frenzied activity. In them worship can become sloppy or sentimental. Teaching can lose its root in the past and become excessively based on the personal experiences of the teacher. A particular "style" of conversion can become the only acceptable kind. And any expression of authority and discipline can be resented. Tom Howard is right up to a point: "Evangelical is not enough."

However, the solution to this problem certainly does not lie in trying to inhibit the evangelical impulse itself. Unfortunately, to her own detriment, the church has not always welcomed the evangelical emphasis which was clearly evident in the New Testament church. During the Great Revival of the eighteenth century, for example, John Wesley was driven out of churches and had to preach in the fields. George Whitefield, an Anglican evangelical

35

like Wesley, was a spell-binding preacher whose
farewell sermon in Boston was heard by 20,000
people. But he was rebuffed by the fashionable
churches in the colonies, and the Harvard faculty
wrote an impressive document voicing their
disapproval — although Benjamin Franklin heard
him gladly. It has often been pointed out that
Methodism never needed to become a separate
denomination, had the Church of England been able
to welcome the outpouring of the Spirit through
these and other prophets of the day.

CHALLENGE

The evangelical challenge has a double edge. From
the church as a whole it asks for leadership which
will stand, as Simeon did, often in isolation and frequently against prevailing trends, and for the kind
of preaching and church life which truly reflects the
New Testament pattern: love for Christ, faithfulness
to his Word, gratitude for salvation, witness to the
world and love for one another. To the individual,
its challenge is very personal. Do we know Christ
as our own Lord and Saviour? Do we so deeply
know his grace that we want to share it with others? Have we ears to listen to his Word with open
hearts, to read/mark/learn/and inwardly digest the
scriptures,[22] and to strengthen one another with
love and good works? If these are our distinguishing

marks, corporately and individually, then it doesn't ultimately matter whether we use the word "evangelical" or others use it of us (in derision or honor), because the evangel will always be the heart of what makes any church a "church."

ENDNOTES

1 Hugh Evan Hopkins, *Charles Simeon of Cambridge* (London: Hodder & Stoughton, 1977).

2 Eph. 4:5; Mt. 16:18; Eph. 5:23; Rom. 8:9-10; Jn. 15:2,10.

3 See *Fearfully and Wonderfully Made, A Surgeon Looks at the Human & Spiritual Body*, Dr. Paul Brand & Philip Yancey (Grand Rapids: Zondervan, 1980), pp.1-67.

4 The Evangelical Education Society, *Outlook* (Winter 1988), p. 5, quoted in *Church Growth and the Power of Evangelism*, Howard Hanchey (Cambridge: Cowley, 1990), p.200.

5 Jude 3.

6 Acts 2:6.

7 Heb. 10:19-25.

8 Heb. 1:1; 3:1; 1:4; 4:14; 1:3.

9 Heb. 4:14; 3:6,14; 10:23.

10 Heb. 13:1-6; 10:26-29.

11 Heb. 11:1-40.

12 Søren Kierkegaard, *Training in Christianity* (Princeton, Princeton University Press: 1957), p. 270-1.

13 Heb. 7:27; 9:12,26; 10:12.

14 2 Ki. 7.

15 *The Journal of the Rev. John Wesley*, Vol. 1, (New York: Dutton Everyman's Library, 1938), p. 102.

16 To discover the continued hold salvation by works has on the ordinary churchgoer, ask the hypothetical question from Evangelism Explosion: "If you were to die tonight and God were to ask you face to face why you should be received into heaven, what would you say?" You will be surprised.

17 Eph. 2:8,9.

18 *The Reform of the Church* (Grand Rapids: Eerdmans, 1970), p.142.

19 Four New Testament quotations (Mt.. 11:28; Jn. 3:16; I Tim. 1:15; I Jn. 2:1, 2) used in Cranmer's service of Holy Communion of 1562 and most subsequent revisions. They were based on Archbishop Hermann's "Consolatio" (1543).

20 Roger Finke and Rodney Stark in *The Churching of America* 1776-1990 (New Brunswick: Rutgers University Press, 1992) point out how dependent early Methodism was on the pastoral gift of laity who acted as exhorters, stewards, and local preachers, as well as class leaders charged with responsibility for the cure of souls. In this way, Methodism was more congregational than Congregationalism, which relied on professional clergy. p. 72-73, 80-81.

21 D.W. Bebbington in *Evangelicalism in Modern Britain, a History from the 1730's to the 1980's* (London: Unwin Hyman, 1989) defines the term evangelicalism by four emphases: conversionism (the exercise of a decisive faith in Christ who justifies sinners); activism (especially in the longing that others be converted); Biblicism (a reverence for the Bible as the only clear and powerful guide to salvation and the primary source of the devotional life); and crucicentrism (the centrality of the substitutionary atonement for theology and holiness), pp. 5-17. I have added a few emphases to his four.

22 From Cranmer's beautiful collect for the Second Sunday in Advent which reflected his desire that the whole Bible be read in public worship year by year. *The Collects, An Introduction an Exposition*, L.E.N. Stephens-Hodge (London: Hodder & Stoughton, 1961) p. 68.

40

Things both old and new

Richard Hooker lived in England from 1554 to 1600 where he served a number of relatively inconsequential parishes. He was a Fellow of Corpus Christi College, Oxford. On the surface, little about his life inspires enthusiasm. His personality was retiring, his appearance was pimply, and his henpecking wife did not help matters. Nevertheless, Hooker has been compared with Shakespeare and Burke in his influence, and praised as a Christian who integrated a protestant head with a catholic heart. Why should this bashful man who hated controversy — and yet wove his way through one of Europe's greatest controversies — be important to our grasp of the church today?

CATHOLIC
The word of continuity and balance

— ◈ ————————————————————

IN THE BOWELS OF Toronto's downtown industrial core sits the parish church of Trinity East, affectionately known as Little Trinity Church. Built by mid-nineteenth century Irish immigrants of fiercely protestant temper, the building in which the congregation worships is the city's oldest surviving church structure. Its appearance reflects the low church theology of the Orangemen who founded it. Visitors, of which the Church has many, are struck at first by the obviously protestant nature of what they see: a preaching hall, with a pulpit figuring prominently above any other feature. At the centre they see a Holy Table (not an altar, please) because Communion is the Lord's Supper, as the Church's sign outside says. A large brass lectern signifies that the public reading of Scripture is a vital part of every service. Bibles in the pews invite worshippers to follow along as the text is read. Visitors on a Sunday see no robed choir, although at times in her past the Church has had one. Moreover, the num-

ber of specifically religious appointments inside the
sanctuary is surprisingly few. Aside from stone and
marble plaques commemorating some of the
Church's early benefactors, which included founders
of one of Canada's great brewing dynasties, visitors
search in vain for memorials to saints or heroes of
the faith. Only soft colored light filters through the
tall, simple stained glass windows. One former
rector used to speak of Little Trinity as having a
"meaningful absence of intended symbolism."

In addition to the architecture, there are other
more important features that mark this Church as
obviously protestant. If one listens carefully, and is
at all familiar with the Bible, it is obvious that all
the theological points in sermons are either implicit
in or derived from Scripture. During announce-
ments, one would hear references to the unusually
large number of home Bible study groups. In some
services, one might encounter free prayer from the
congregation; and one would probably notice that
laity participate in almost every aspect of the worship service. The focus of worship is intentionally
on the Word of God: Jesus as the Word incarnate,
the Bible as the word written, preaching as the
Word expounded, and the sacraments as the word
made visible.

Certainly one of the most notably protestant
Anglican churches in Canada, Little Trinity has
architectural parallels in many historic Episcopal

churches in the United States, whose interiors are dominated by central pulpits and where the communion table is almost invisible![1]

BUT IS IT PROTESTANT ONLY?

However, among the church's visitors, some of whom eventually become parishioners, there are those who are struck by how catholic we appear. Having been brought up Presbyterian, Baptist, Mennonite, Independent, or Brethren, they notice such things as the gothic revival architecture of our building. They take note of our liturgical worship, our adherence to the traditional Christian Year with its seasons of Advent, Epiphany, Lent, Easter, and Pentecost. They notice how frequently we celebrate Holy Communion, and with what reverence, and they are aware that the Holy Table, not the pulpit, is the central piece of furniture in the Church. They notice that the clergy are robed in vestments rather than dressed in business suits or academic gowns, and that we preserve the historic three orders of ministry: bishops, priests, and deacons. They spot the bishop's chair against the back wall, with a mitre carved into it. And if they happen to be among us on the date of his visit, they see that the bishop is received with dignity, affection, and respect. His pastoral letters are read to the congregation. They might notice that we stand when the Gospel is read, recite the Creeds during both Morning Prayer and Holy Communion services, and pass the ancient Christian greeting of the Peace as a sign of our reconciliation with one another. They are very aware that we practice infant baptism, and make the sign of the cross on the brow of the baptized. To these non-Anglicans our church appears distinctly catholic. All of which raises the question: Is this a protestant or a catholic Church?

BRITAIN BEFORE THE REFORMATION

History helps us to answer this question by reminding us that before the Anglican Church was the Church *of* England, it was, first of all, the church *in* England. There Christianity traces itself back to the Celts who were evangelized in the second century by missionaries from Gaul. Soon these Celtic Christians in England were sending missionaries out to the further reaches of the British isles. Men like Patrick, Ninian, and Columba spread the Gospel to Ireland and Scotland.

In the fifth century, when pagan Angles and Saxons invaded Britain, the Celts were driven to the fringes of the land. Undaunted by this setback, they soon set about the conversion of the Angles and Saxons, led by Aidan, who in turn was helped by Augustine of Canterbury and other missionaries from Rome. With these new missionaries came Roman customs and Roman church government.

During the Middle Ages and Renaissance, the success and subsequent wealth of the church in Britain encouraged a number of abuses. Worldly minded kings and powerful Popes vied for influence and control. Clergy became morally corrupt and spiritually indifferent. Monasteries amassed riches and exuded luxury. Theologians overlaid the Gospel with unbiblical speculations, and the laity were ignorant and superstitious. Reform became absolutely necessary.

TURBULENCE AND REFORM

After the English civil war of the 15th century, King Henry VIII desperately wanted a male heir so his Tudor dynasty could keep England intact. The inevitable break with Rome (over his divorce of Queen Katherine, who, he believed, would never produce a son) gave those church leaders in Britain who were interested in reform the chance they were looking for. Reforms which had already become widely adopted on the Continent were given the backing of some leading bishops and theologians and, to a certain degree, of Henry himself, in a vacillating fashion. After Henry's death, great strides towards European Protestantism were made by zealous university theologians and, unfortunately, cynical politicians. The subsequent death of his sickly son Edward led to terrifying setbacks during the reign of the infamous "Bloody Mary," Henry's daughter by Katherine, who was determined to restore Roman Catholicism by force. But after Mary's death, Elizabeth, Henry's second daughter, came to the throne. As the daughter of Anne Boleyn, for whom Henry had divorced Katherine, Elizabeth had a strong political interest, apart from any other consideration, in maintaining the Reformation — the powerful Roman Catholic princes of Europe considered her illegitimate and believed that she had no right of succession to the English throne. With her firm support, the basic ideas of the Reformation became incorporated into the Church of England forever.

Had you entered an English church of Elizabeth's day, you would have seen an interior very much like what visitors see in many of the "lower" Anglican churches around the world today: a freestanding Holy Table rather than a stone altar, a Bible in English rather than Latin, and clergy robed in a black scarf over a white surplice rather than in richly decorated vestments. Crucifixes would have been rare, processions minimal, and prayers for the departed used with restraint, if at all. Sermons would have reflected Reformation theological insights; and the priest, instead of elevating the consecrated bread and wine, would offer it to the people as a means of grace and spiritual feeding.

Of course, many Anglican churches, in response to the Anglo-Catholic Oxford Movement of the last century, have reintroduced many of the external trappings of the medieval church which the Reformers set aside.[2] In fact, within Anglicanism, from the earliest days, the pendulum has always swung between those who wished to revive many medieval customs dropped at the Reformation and those who felt that the simple ceremonial resulting from the Reformation was all that was needed.

BOTH PROTESTANT AND CATHOLIC

Nevertheless, whether it uses a great deal of ceremonial and ornamentation or very little, the Anglican Church lays claim to being both protestant and catholic. It has preserved much more of the order, ceremony, and sacramental focus of the historic church than many protestant churches do. But it embraced the theology, the Scriptural authority, and the spirituality of the Reformation.

For Anglicans and others, it may be helpful to recall that the word "protestant" did not originally mean anti-catholic, as it now tends to mean in the popular mind. When first used in 1529, and for more than a century thereafter, the word "protestant" meant a declaration of intent to abide by God's Word alone as the sure rule of doctrine and conduct and as the unfailing test of all that is true and good. A protestation was a solemn declaration for something. Only secondarily did it mean a protest against the errors supported and encouraged by the Papacy.[3]

The origin of the word "catholic" goes back to the second century A.D. when Ignatius said in a letter that "where Jesus Christ is present, we have the catholic Church." The value of the church being "catholic" lies in the important emphases that it preserves. Specifically, this value is rooted in what the word tells us about the sovereignty of God.

First, the word "catholic" witnesses to the belief that God has been sovereign over the development of his church since the very beginning. When Jesus promised that the Gates of Hell would not prevail against his church, he meant, I think, both that Satan would not eliminate the church, and that his Spirit would not abandon the church. This promise, though undoubtedly linked to the church's ongoing obedience, was not dependent on it. God is sovereign and his plan for those who would join Jesus in the fellowship of the new covenant would stand — even if the church at times was unfaithful to him. When we confess in the Apostles' Creed our faith in "the one, holy, catholic and apostolic church" we are saying that the church that we believe in is the historic church that has existed throughout the centuries. It is neither simply a private construct in our own minds of what the church ought to be nor merely an organization currently on the scene that can be described sociologically. We confess that, despite corruption and frequent error, the historic church is nonetheless God's church.

Secondly, the word "catholic" recognizes that the Bible and the Church have a special relationship to each other. Since it was the Apostolic preaching contained in the Bible that created the Church, the Church must never be seen as "over" the Bible. To the contrary, the Church is "under" the Bible, in the sense that the Church must bow to the authority of the Bible. However, the Church is the "witness and keeper of holy Writ," as the Thirty-Nine Articles say. In terms of understanding, interpreting, and relating the Bible to current issues and controversies, God has sovereignly worked through the Church to give us light. Therefore, our use of the word "catholic" to describe the church recognizes that the church's great tradition of interpreting and understanding the Bible is from God. While this does not sanctify any aspect of that tradition as infallible, it gives us a deep respect for those with a wisdom greater than ourselves and a presumption in favor of their understanding over subsequent insights (and especially over novel insights). Thus, Tradition is not over Scripture, and not even alongside Scripture as an equal. Rather, it is the lens through which the early church read Scripture. It is a gift from the past which helps to illuminate the present.

Thirdly, the word "catholic" acknowledges that God has sovereignly worked through his church, even though its diversity has often appeared to be chaos. The church, with its wide variety of rites and ceremonies, its different forms of church government, its different interpretations of Bible particulars, and its contrasting ways of relating to the established powers, has nonetheless been a vehicle of grace to the many who have found shelter in its wings. "Catholic" is therefore a comprehensive word. It affirms that where the Creeds are upheld, the Scriptures honored, the Word of God proclaimed, and the sacraments rightly practiced, there is the church.[4]

BOTH VISIBLE AND INVISIBLE

Such inclusiveness has posed problems for Christians who wanted to distinguish those within the church who were only nominal Christians from those who were committed Christians. Therefore some Christians, including Cranmer and other Anglican theologians in the sixteenth and seventeenth centuries, spoke of the "invisible church," referring to those within the wider body who are truly saved. By the use of this phrase they did not mean that there were two churches — a visible one and an invisible one. Rather they meant that the one church exists in two states or conditions: "Now visible and invisible maketh not two Churches; but the divers estate and condition of the same Church," said Richard Hooker in the sixteenth century.[5] Since both wheat and tares are to be found within the kingdom, they insisted, with Jesus, that it is not up to us to separate the two from each other here on earth.

Thus, the word "catholic" bears witness to the conviction that God has not abandoned his Church. Even in its darkest periods, there have been a thousand points of light. God has guided a tradition of understanding the Scriptures which belongs to us all. And God has permitted himself to be honored in a great variety of ways within the basic framework of orthodoxy.

Just how broad, though, should the net be when we use the word "catholic"? Roman Catholics restrict the word to themselves and to Eastern Orthodoxy. They, in fact, do not even recognize Anglican orders as legitimate, although since Vatican II Anglicans, together with all protestants, are referred to as "separated brethren." On the Anglican side of the Reformation divide, however, the whole church is included in the word "catholic" — protestant, catholic, Orthodox and Pentecostal.

The four essentials

While Anglicans seek to be as inclusive as possible, they do nevertheless hold that four things rightly belong to the Church as a whole. These four things, which were first articulated in Chicago in 1886, and soon afterwards adopted by the Lambeth Conference, should be part of any scheme for re-union between separated churches. So, for instance, when the Church of South India was created in 1947, a Church in which Anglican, Presbyterian, Congregational, and Lutheran churches were united, these four things were agreed upon as essential:

• First, the Holy Scriptures of the Old and New Testaments are accepted as "containing all things necessary to salvation" and as being the rule and ultimate standard of faith.

• Second, the Apostles' Creed is accepted as the baptismal symbol and the Nicene Creed as the sufficient statement of the Christian faith. Both teach us how to read scripture.

• Third, the two sacraments as ordained by Christ himself —baptism and the supper of the Lord — ministered with unfailing use of Christ's word of institution, and of the elements (of bread and wine) ordained by him.

• Fourth, the historic episcopate, locally adapted in the methods of its administration to the varying needs of the nations and people called of God into the unity of his Church.

This last point is the controversial one, raising as it does the question of whether Anglicans believe (along with Roman Catholics) that, without bishops, there is no church. Despite the fact that in the first few centuries, before the canon of Scripture was fixed, bishops served an absolutely crucial function as keepers of orthodoxy, such a view, where held, is highly divisive and without scriptural support. Consequently, it has never been official Anglican teaching. The teaching is rather that bishops are meant to be the sign of unity for the whole church. If episcopacy (oversight) were shared, argues Henry Chadwick, nothing fundamental to the church would be lost. But there is a practical need for the expression of unity, and bishops fulfill that need.[6] Since there is solid New Testament evidence for bishops[7] and since they have undeniable pastoral value, Anglicans are not prepared to set aside that part of the church's heritage in any proposed re-union scheme.[8]

A MIDDLE WAY

Because it was historically the via media between Roman Catholicism and the radical Protestants[9], the Anglican church has sought to read Scripture with a careful, balanced, non-dogmatic mind. This is also part of that catholicity of viewpoint which has sought to approach the text for what it says rather than for what we hope it says. To see how this works, consider the following passage and join me in attempting to look at it with catholic, as opposed to Roman Catholic or militantly Protestant, eyes:

> Is any among you suffering? Let him pray. Is any cheerful? Let him sing praise. Is any among you sick? Let him call for the elders of the church, and let them pray over him, anointing him with oil in the name of the Lord; and the prayer of faith will save the sick man, and the Lord will raise him up; and if he has committed sins, he will be forgiven. Therefore confess your sins to one another, and pray for one another, that you may be healed. The prayer of a righteous man has great power in its effects. Elijah was a man of like nature with ourselves and he prayed fervently that it might not rain, and for three years and six months it did not rain on the earth. Then he prayed again and the heaven gave rain, and the earth brought forth its fruit.[10]

Someone in the early church is seriously sick. The elders are called. But who are these elders? The Roman Catholic Church's official translation of the Bible into English, the Douay version, says that the people called are priests. However, nowhere is the Greek word for a sacrificing priest (*hiereus*) to be found in the text, or for that matter anywhere in the New Testament, as a reference to Christian ministers. Roman Catholics are on shaky ground in their identification of New Testament ministers with the priests of the Old Testament. The origin of their view is that, as Christ was both priest and victim in offering himself, so his apostles — and by extension all anointed through them for ministry — share in Christ's eternal priesthood. The word for priest in the Anglican Church is a transliteration of the Greek word *presbyteros*, meaning "elder." While later apologists like Urban T. Holmes attempt to read into Anglican usage a sacrificing priesthood on the theory that the priest recalls or represents the one sufficient sacrifice of Christ to the Father, they have to admit that this was not original Anglican teaching.[11] Over against the Roman Catholic reading of this text, and quite possibly in reaction to it, one encounters the strictly protestant reading: these elders are the pastors and lay leaders who are the duly authorized rulers of the Church.[12]

But how might a catholic (with a small "c") read this passage? One would begin by singling out the fact that the church as a whole is asked to have a role in the healing of the sick. Within the church, a group is seen to have the spiritual authority and the gifts to help the sick by visiting them and praying for them. One might lay stress on the fact that those called were not necessarily office holders as much as they were ordinary people of faith who, like Elijah, lived righteous lives and whose prayers were earnest and powerful.

Then James says that these people are to anoint the sick person with oil. What is the meaning of this? Roman Catholics take this to mean "consecrated oil"; hence, they find in this text justification for the sacrament of Extreme Unction, the anointing of dying or seriously ill persons. In an approved Roman Catholic edition of the Bible, a footnote to this verse says that it teaches "in the plainest terms" that "previously consecrated oil is an effective medium of forgiveness in the case of those who are no longer able to make conscious confession of sin and receive priestly absolution."[13] The Roman Catholic reading must be seen as tendentious here, because nowhere does the passage envision death as the outcome. Rather, the expectation is that the sick person will be fully restored to health by the prayers of the righteous.

Contrast this with the strictly protestant reading which sees the oil here not as sacramental but as medicinal. Protestant interpreters have pointed to the fact that oil was one of the most commonly used medicines in biblical times, that the Good Samaritan poured oil into the wounds of the man by the road, and that the word for "anoint" here is "to daub or smear," not the word for ritual anointing.

As a catholic with a small "c," I cannot see the text as a justification for Extreme Unction because, as I indicated above, contrary to the Roman Catholic reading, death is not envisioned here, but full restoration to health. Jesus never instituted such a sacrament, as the Thirty-Nine Articles rightly say. Nor do I think that the extreme protestant view that the oil is (merely) medicinal goes to the heart of the interpretation. It would appear rather that the Holy Spirit is being invoked under the sign of oil, and that James is saying that, just as the Apostles anointed with oil and healed many, so Christians should open themselves up to the Lord's healing power through the outward sign of oil, when accompanied by sincere faith. Here then is testimony to a very early practice in which outward signs were taken to be deeply helpful to the life of faith.

CONFESS YOUR SINS

Finally, there is the matter of confession. Reading "priests" for elders in this passage, Roman Catholics understand the phrase "confess your sins to one another" as support for auricular confession — private confession to a priest, who alone has the power to grant absolution. On the other hand, I have heard some protestant enthusiasts read this verse as an instruction to the people to confess their sins publicly to each other as a kind of catharsis which enables the Spirit to work more freely.

Again, a catholic with a small "c," reads this verse differently: The person to whom one should confess is the one who has been wronged. Nothing is said here either about confession to a priest, or about

58

public confession. Without being overly dogmatic, I believe that a (small "c") catholic reading of this passage would point to the obvious link that the New Testament makes between sickness and sin. While there is, of course, no necessary causal connection between sickness and sin, there is nonetheless a scriptural basis for asking every believer who wishes healing to seek forgiveness from any whom they have wronged so that things that might hinder God's grace within are acknowledged and, by God's grace, put aside.

A catholic view of Scripture thus helps save us from certain extremes. Specifically, it seeks to avoid interpretations that justify beliefs and practices that have not been received by the church as a whole. Therefore, the catholic avoids the dogmatic Roman Catholic reading of this passage and the reactionary protestant reading as well.

THE GREAT SYSTEMATICIAN

The catholic Christian whom I admire perhaps above all is Richard Hooker. For all of his unremarkable qualities, he stood out, in the opinion of many, in wisdom. Hooker lived at a time when a radical group of Puritans in the Church of England wanted to do away with what few vestiges of catholicism remained in the post-Reformation Church. They wanted a church purified of everything that could not be explicitly deduced from Scripture.

They were not interested in the insights of the early Fathers, the thought of the medieval scholars, or the outer trappings of ceremonial. They wanted a church without liturgy, without bishops, and without a Prayer Book. To them, the Book of Common Prayer was "an imperfect book, culled and picked out of that popish dunghill the mass book [which was] full of abominations."

It was Hooker who rose to the defense of a balanced Reformation. He embraced Reformation theology and was strong on the supreme authority of the Bible and on justification by faith alone. But he balanced this by recognizing the philosophers, theologians, and liturgical scholars of the past as true Christians — even though they may have erred on certain points. Hooker saw a place for both reason and tradition in the ongoing life of the Church, even though he believed them to be subordinate to Scripture:

> What Scripture doth plainly deliver it is that the first place both of credit and obedience is due; the next whereunto is whatsoever any man can necessarily conclude by force of reason. After these the voice of the Church succeedeth.[14]

While admitting much of the Puritan case, Hooker believed that the outward forms of worship or church government were "things indifferent" —

things that might be changed if circumstances required. Hooker avoided enshrining antiquity; but he esteemed it nonetheless.

His great work, *The Laws of Ecclesiastical Polity*, was a creative masterpiece, synthesizing all the best of the past with the fresh insights of the Reformation. Hooker preserved Anglicanism from both the radical Puritans and the conservative Romanizers, using reason as a weapon against the former and Scripture as a weapon against the latter. He saw that the Anglican Reformation was not itself a principle to be idealized and pressed into some utopian vision. For example, the radical protestants sought to purify the visible church, insisting that only those whose profession and life were unquestionably sanctified be included; therefore, they questioned infant baptism. But Hooker argued that the church will always contain some who eat and drink the body and blood of Christ to their own damnation. Here on earth the church will always be prone to err, and therefore to be in need of reform. To quote a modern sage, the church is more a hospital for sinners than a museum for saints! Of the apostasy in the days of Elijah, Hooker wrote:

> ... amongst them God always had his Church, because he had thousands which never bowed their knees to Baal; but those whose knees *were* bowed unto Baal, even they were also of the visible Church of God.[15]

Instead of a utopian vision, the Anglican Reformation was a correction, a way to bring the Church back into harmony with its own neglected past and with the teachings of Scripture. Hooker has been compared with greats like Shakespeare and Burke. He would have blanched at such comparisons, and insisted that he was just a modest cleric bringing out of the storehouse of his mind things both old and new.[16]

We may be thankful for this modest man, and for all who, like him, have helped preserve the church in forms that have Scriptural integrity. Because of him and others, we may avoid the narrow sectarian thinking that exalts one branch of Christendom as if it were the whole vine. We are able to see ourselves as simply one part of the "one, holy, catholic, and apostolic" Church.

ENDNOTES

1 Trinity Church, Newport, RI; St. Peter's, Society Hill, PA; Bruton Parish, Williamsburg, VA — to name just a few.

2 Scholars point to the influence of John Mason Neal, Anglican author and hymnwriter (1818-1866) who, with B. Webb, founded the Cambridge Camden Society which, through its periodical, *The Ecclesiologist*, greatly encouraged the readoption of medieval liturgical practices, dress, and architecture.

3 Peter Toon, *The Anglican Way*, Evangelical and Catholic (Wilton: Morehouse-Barlow, 1983), p. 70.

4 The Reformed family of churches is said to conceive of the church as the people of God, the sacramental churches to think of it as the body of Christ, and the pentecostal churches to regard it as the fellowship of the Spirit. See Lesslie Newbigin, *The Household of God* (London: SCM Press, 1953). Edmund Clowney comments, "No doubt all are in danger of ignoring the rich balance of the biblical revelation, and ... of focusing on one figure exclusively." *The Doctrine of the Church* (Philadelphia: Presbyterian and Reformed, 1969), p. 10.

5 Attributed to Richard Hooker by William Covell in *Just and Temperate Defense of the Five Books of Ecclesiastical Polity* (London, 1603), p.70. Quoted in John S. Marshall, *Hooker and the Anglican Tradition* (London: Adam & Charles Black, 1963), p. 156.

6 Henry Chadwick, "Episcopacy in the New Testament and Early Church" in *Today's Church* and *Today's World*, ed. John Howe (CIO 1977), pp. 211-212.

7 I Tim.3:1; 2 Tim. 1:7; Phil. 1:1. Some argue that these texts, while mentioning bishops, do not distinguish between bishops and presbyters, and thus do not imply a clear threefold structure to the ministry (bishops, presbyters, and deacons). Others

reply that bishops were indeed presbyters, but some bishops from very early days functioned as "first among equals."

8 The Lambeth Quadrilateral. See *The Study of Anglicanism*, Stephen Sykes and John Booty, eds. (London/Minneapolis: SPCK/Fortress, 1988), p. 232.

9 It is often falsely asserted that Anglicanism is the middle way between Catholicism and Protestantism. In fact, many Puritans were part of mainstream Anglicanism in the period between 1560 and 1640 and were content to live under episcopacy, provided there was biblical preaching and some degree of freedom in the Spirit. It was a small group of unrepresentative Puritan hotheads, like John Field and Walter Travers, say scholars like Patrick Collinson, Peter Lake, and Nicholas Tyalke, who rejected Anglicanism *in toto*. Therefore, says church historian Leslie Fairfield, "It's been established that the Anglican *via media* runs between Rome and Anabaptism, not between Rome and Puritanism — that the Anglican 'middle way' of the Elizabethan Settlement (and for the next 80 years) was a variety of Reformed Protestantism, and not a strand of Christianity distinct from the latter."

10 Jas. 5:13-18.

11 Urban T. Holmes III, *What is Anglicanism?* (Toronto: Anglican Book Centre, 1982), p. 54-5.

12 *The Expositors Bible Commentary*, Frank E. Gaebelein, ed. Vol. 12, A commentary on James, Donald W. Burdick, (Grand Rapids: Zondervan, 1981), p. 203.

13 R.V.G. Tasker, James, *An Introduction and Commentary* (London: Tyndale Press, 1956), p. 128-131.

14 *Ecclesiastical Polity*, Book V, Chapter 8, Section II.

15 Ibid., Book III, Chapter 1, Section VII. (emphasis added)

16 J.R.H. Moorman, *A History of the Church in England* (New York: Morehouse-Barlow, 1959) p. 215-16, 225.

66

Shaken to its roots

Hugh Latimer (1485-1555) was the preacher
and propagandizer of the English Reformation.
A contemporary of Archbishop Cranmer who
composed the Book of Common Prayer, Latimer
was a Fellow of Clare College, Cambridge; Rector of a church in the diocese of Salisbury; then
Bishop of Worcester — and finally martyr. He
advised kings and heralded the gospel (from the
back of his horse) to common men. He was both
an agitator and a victim of the turbulent years
when the Church of England was shaken to its
roots. What were his concerns as he looked at
the church of his day, and why is his reforming
vision still needed in the church of ours?

REFORMED
The word of freedom
and truth

— ✝ ————————————————

Thomas was so small that his friends had nicknamed him "Little Bilney"; but within his small body was a fiery heart that burned with a passion for truth. As he listened to the great Cambridge lecturer hold forth with brilliance and charm on the errors of Melanchthon, a noted Continental Reformer, he thought to himself that the one who spoke with such conviction might not be as convinced in his heart as his words would indicate.

Thus it was that Thomas Bilney asked Hugh Latimer to hear his confession. Surprised but willing to oblige, Latimer suggested that Bilney accompany him to the confessional box. We will never know precisely what transpired in that confessional, but it was a conversation that ignited the English Reformation. Bilney shared his struggle over sin and his discovery of the grace of God in such a way that Latimer later wrote: "Master Bilney ... was the instrument whereby God called me to knowledge; for I may thank him next to God for that knowledge that I have in the Word of God."[1]

Latimer soon rose to become the English Reformation's greatest champion, preaching to kings and, in the open air, to crowds of common folk. He helped raise up a nation of preachers who could talk, not in academic jargon, but in the language of the people. Fearless, he was unhesitating in his attacks on "unpreaching prelates who are so troubled with lordly living, rustling in their rents, dancing in their dominions, pampering their paunches, munching in their mangers, and loitering in their lordship, that they cannot attend to preaching."

He was a man whose fortunes were destined to wax and wane in relation to political changes in the nation. During the reign of Henry VIII, he was in favor — but only just. He was installed as Bishop of Worcester; but later thrown into the Tower of London on suspicion of heresy. He was released but had to promise not to preach. Then, when Edward VI came to the throne he was set free. Although well on in years, he travelled the length of the land preaching the Gospel and he was greatly revered by all. When Mary came to the throne, determined to reestablish Roman Catholicism by any means, Latimer was imprisoned again, this time together with bishops Ridley and Cranmer.

THE MEDIEVAL MUDDLE

Part of the difficulty of church reform in the later Middle Ages was the intermingling of theology and politics, religion and society. You could not touch one without affecting the other. The structures of the church had, over a period of at least 500 years, become indistinguishable from the feudal society with which it coexisted and in which it was by far the largest single cultural influence.

In those days, wealth was measured in land. The church had inherited an immense amount of property, ironically, through wealthy men and women who had given it to the church so that they could live a simple, monastic life. At one point it is said that the church owned as much as half of all the territory of France and Germany. Popes were consequently enormously wealthy. For instance, during the period in which the papacy was located at Avignon (1309-78), the Popes collected an income three times that of the king of France. Pope John XXII devised an ingenious scheme to fill his coffers: he instituted a rule, called the annate, whereby the first year's income of any bishop must go to the pope. Thus, when money was needed for this project or that, a transfer of bishops was arranged so that a vacancy could be created and thereby a handsome windfall was engineered for the papacy. This worked so well that an even better plan was devised: leave an episcopal see vacant for a few years, and appropriate all the revenue! Nor were the Renaissance popes any improvement on their medieval predecessors. On the whole, they were worldly, indolent, mercenary, impious, and rarely even celibate! Conveniently, church teaching distinguished the office of the papacy from its holder, and therefore the Pope's claim to infallibility did not rest on his impeccability.[2]

Because it was common for bishops to live off the incomes of their substantial land holdings and never to lay eyes on the dioceses in their charge, clergy were left to their own devices. They were often uneducated and spiritually indifferent, and so the laity got by on popular speculation rather than sound teaching from the scriptures. Much of this speculation centered on the terrors of "purgatory" and how to avoid them. As a result, a huge business in the sale of indulgences arose, aimed at capitalizing on this anxiety. These indulgences were based on the dubious principle that since the saints had more righteousness than was needed for their own salvation, ordinary mortals could be credited with some of their righteousness. This transfer of merits enabled purchasers to avoid lengthy stays in purgatory after they died, and thus hastened their progress towards salvation.

Monasteries, which also became centers of great wealth, were often similarly corrupted. Monasticism obviously was in need of a major overhaul. Roland H. Bainton described the monastic spiral this way: Discipline begat abundance, and abundance destroyed discipline; and discipline in its fall pulled down abundance.[3] Fortunately, there were reformers like St. Francis of Assisi and others, who lived sacrificial lives in primitive areas of Europe. But they were often ignored.

To the zealous and scholarly John Wycliffe (1329-84), English monks in the 14th century were "fat cows" with "red cheeks and great bellies", living useless lives surrounded by sumptuousness and languishing in spiritual stupor. With ready pen and biting wit, he called for the disendowment of the monasteries and the confiscation of church property. Often seen as the "Morning Star" of the Reformation, Wycliffe used his considerable scholarship to draw attention to theological errors in medieval doctrine. Furthermore, he helped inspire later bands of "Poor Preachers" who, despite danger and hardship, travelled the length and breadth of the land preaching the gospel and urging people to read the Bible for themselves.[4] Yet he was not willing to break from the Church.

CRY FOR REFORM

Abuses like these cried out for structural reform, and it is no wonder that throughout the centuries preceding the Reformation there were significant voices of protest, like those of Wycliffe in England

and Huss on the continent. But it was not just structural reform that was needed; theological reform
was also necessary. This is where Latimer and others
in England linked arms with their continental counterparts. The medieval cycle of redemption focused
on the sacraments because they were believed to
confer salvation. First, a person was baptized. By
this rite, all previous sin was washed away, and the
person was entitled to membership in the Christian
Church, with all its attendant privileges. With so
much hinging on baptism, of course nearly every
child was baptized. Then, to deal with ongoing sins,
the church provided penance, which was effective as
long as sins were confessed to a priest who alone
had the power to absolve them. The heart of the
sacramental cycle focused on the sacrament of the
Mass which could be counted on to propitiate God's
wrath because it repeatedly offered Christ's death to
the Father in the consecrated bread and wine. From
the moment the words of institution were uttered
over these consecrated elements — "This is my body
… this is my blood" — they were now no longer
mere bread and wine, they were the actual body
and blood of Christ and therefore could be resacri-
ficed in a bloodless way as an offering to the Father.
Mere attendance at Mass was understood by the
people to effect reconciliation with God for the time
being. In the end, at the point of death, since there
was still uncertainty about the effectiveness of all

that had gone before, a final sacrament was needed to erase any still unconfessed sins. With the provision of Extreme Unction, the cycle was complete.

The weight of this was enormous when applied to the life of the seriously religious person. There were no guarantees of salvation, even if the cycle was completed, because one could never be sure that one had amassed sufficient merit to be saved. Moreover, there were always sins which one might have forgotten. Many labored under the burden of this system, but few as much as a young German Augustinian monk named Martin Luther. He was one of the first to publish his convictions about the oppressiveness of this system, with the help of the recent invention of the printing press.

Luther began by questioning whether there really ever had been such a thing as superfluous merit that could be transferred from the saints to someone else. He reasoned that if sin was as serious as he knew in his experience it was, then how could any saint have amassed more than he or she needed? This shook Luther's faith in the whole medieval system. But it left him full of anxiety. How, without the merits of others, could anyone possibly do enough on their own? Luther decided to try. He became a monk; he fasted, made repeated confessions, mortified the flesh, engaged in endless prayer vigils, and tried all manner of austerity, but in all this, he failed to find the needed assurance. One day he had to conclude that, instead of loving God, he really hated God — this God who only made him feel more and more condemned.

FREE AT LAST

It was the Bible that finally brought peace to Luther's soul. Studying it diligently in order to give some lectures to his students, he discovered the true meaning of justification. It was a revelation to him that justification was not earned by keeping the law, but rather it was a gift given by grace to those who have faith in Jesus Christ. Once his eyes were opened, Luther found this doctrine everywhere in the Bible, especially in the works of St. Paul. Passages like this jumped out at him:

> We ourselves, who are Jews by birth and not Gentile sinners, yet who know that a man is not justified by works of the law but through faith in Jesus Christ, even we have believed in Christ Jesus, in order to be justified by faith in Christ, and not by works of the law, because by works of the law shall no one be justified. But if, in our endeavor to be justified in Christ, we ourselves were found to be sinners, is Christ then an agent of sin? Certainly not! But if I build up again those things which I tore down, then I prove myself a transgressor. For I through the law died to the law, that I might live to God. I have been crucified with Christ; it is no longer I who live, but Christ who lives in me; and the life I now

live in the flesh I live by faith in the Son of God, who loved me and gave himself for me. I do not nullify the grace of God; for if justification were through the law, then Christ died to no purpose.[5]

JUSTIFICATION BY FAITH

What Luther discovered through these and other Scriptures was that the law was never intended to make one just or righteous in God's sight. The law brings only death — a sense of futility. No one had known this better than St. Paul who, as Saul of Tarsus, had tried to be justified by the law, and failed. To "build up again those things which I tore down", says Paul in the passage above, would be to reinstitute the law as a means of gaining justification. Such an action denies the Gospel and spreads a sense of condemnation to everyone. As Luther pondered this, he concluded that this was just what the medieval church was doing!

But Luther saw that Christ on the cross had taken the condemnation which Luther deserved upon himself and had given us his righteousness, so that we might receive it as a gift through faith. Thus Christ's death was a death to the law; and when he died, we who are united to him by faith, died also. Therefore, the law no longer has a claim upon us for justification. We can go free, just as if we had never sinned. We become new people, born again to a life in union with a God who loved us so much as to take all our condemnation and give all his righteousness in return.

In his commentary on Romans 1:16-17, Luther expressed his joy in this discovery:

> Night and day I pondered until I saw the connection be-
> tween the justice of God and the statement that "the just
> shall live by faith." Then I grasped that the justice of God
> is that righteousness by which through grace and sheer
> mercy God justifies us through faith. Thereupon I felt
> myself to be reborn and to have gone through open
> doors into paradise. The whole of Scripture took on a
> new meaning, and whereas before the "justice of God"
> had filled me with hate, now it became to me inexpress-
> ibly sweet in greater love. This passage of Paul became
> to me a gate to heaven.

Justification by faith became the anvil on which the Reformation was shaped. Luther wrote of it: "This is the truth of the gospel. It is also the principal article of all Christian doctrine, wherein the knowledge of all godliness consisteth." "This is the doctrine which maketh true Christians indeed."[6]

FINE TUNING THE TRUTH

But justification was a doctrine that needed precise definition. What is the relation between Christ's righteousness and ours? This question has divided Christendom ever since Luther grasped the fact of justification by faith and exposed the fallacy in the medieval cycle of redemption. Luther and the other reformers, both Continental and Anglican, said that we receive justification as a legal act. That is, we are counted or declared righteous before the bar of God. Christ's righteousness is credited to our account, and thus we are forgiven and — through faith — united to Christ and now desire to live for his glory.

The Roman Catholics of the day refused to accept this legal metaphor, saying that we receive Christ's righteousness not as a credit to our account, but as an inward experience. We receive it as a grace partly in response to our good works (including the good work of faith) and partly in response to our participation in the sacraments. To the Catholic, the believer is not counted righteous, but made righteous. Instead of being a legal act, justification is an inward change which makes us acceptable to God. The Council of Trent's Decree on Justification (1547) said that "They, through the observance of the commandments of God and of the Church, faith co-operating with good works, increase in that justice which they have received through the grace of Christ, ... are still further justified."[7]

In the post-Vatican-II era of ecumenical dialogue, many Roman Catholic writers (and some Protestants too) have tried to overcome the stark antithesis of these two views. Hans Kung, for instance, admits the scriptural basis of the legal metaphor, but finally comes down on the side of saying that justification includes making us righteous.[8] He follows the pattern set down by John Henry Newman, who began as an Anglican and turned Roman Catholic. Newman tried desperately to have it both ways, recognizing that the biblical term "justify" means to "count" righteous, but insisting that "justify" must also mean that we become righteous by the indwelling Spirit.[9] This watershed, to this very day, separates Reformed from Catholic theology. Many Anglicans and other Protestants look for a clearer repudiation in post-Vatican-II Roman Catholic teaching of the idea that justification is an inward change which makes us righteous before God.[10]

But to the Reformers, and to reformed thinkers today, justification by faith is the key that unlocks not only theology but spirituality as well. For what is sanctification essentially but applied justification? Real holiness grows out of an awareness of how wonderful it is to be forgiven, how much love we owe to our Saviour, how abundant is his grace, and how free we are to obey the law which once was the source of our condemnation. The Reformers saw that to read St. Paul as meaning that justification was an inward change, in which we actually become righteous and therefore acceptable, was to misread him. It was to reintroduce the whole medieval system of gaining merits by good works and of having grace infused into us automatically by the sacraments. Only through justification by faith is all the glory given to God; for it is God alone who saves us by his grace. Without it we are simply pleading our own goodness before the throne. Rooted in this wonderful discovery are the three watchwords of the Reformation: *sola fide* (by faith alone), *sola gratia* (by grace alone), and *soli Deo gloria* (to God alone be glory). Many added a fourth watchword, *sola scriptura*, because it is from the Scriptures that we learn these truths.

THE RELATIONSHIP BETWEEN FAITH AND WORKS

To Luther and all the Reformers, justification by faith alone was the article on which the church stood or fell. Fortunately, our Anglican Reformers, like Latimer, stood solidly with him and with the other Continental Reformers in affirming justification by faith. They took pains to write it into the Thirty-Nine Articles of Religion which are found at the back of the Anglican Prayer Book. No fewer than eight Articles relate directly or indirectly to justification. For example,

> We are accounted righteous before God, only on the merit of our Lord and Saviour Jesus Christ by Faith, and not for our own works or deservings: Wherefore, that we are justified by faith only is a most wholesome Doctrine, and very full of comfort ... (Article XI)

Whenever this doctrine is taught, someone is bound to object that if we are justified by faith — that is counted, declared (literally in the Greek "worded") righteous — why should we bother with good works? Paul knew the question well: "Is Christ, then, an agent of sin?" he asks the Galatians. His answer to them was twofold. First, faith unites us in a new life with Jesus Christ. Since his life is now at work in us, that new life will bring with it those loving acts by which real faith is always known. Second, the Spirit of Christ within now leads us and enables us to live a life of obedience to God's laws — out of freedom rather than out of a fear of condemnation. Paul is careful to explain that "by the works of the law shall no flesh be justified." But he is also clear that once justification has been received, we are now freed from the endless cycle of self-justification to "live to God." Justification remains a legal act, but it necessarily leads onward to a life of sanctification.

HOLINESS IN DAILY LIFE

It is in this area of sanctification that we owe a great debt to the second stream of the Reformation, that which flowed from the work of John Calvin. Calvin's *Institutes of the Christian Religion*, originally subtitled *Containing the whole sum of piety*, were aimed at taking the practical holiness which the medieval system relegated to the seriously religious only, by which it meant those in monastic life, and relating it to ordinary believers who lived in the world. Every Christian, said Calvin, was to have a vocation from God and to be holy. Every Christian was to engage in warfare with the powers of evil, mortify the flesh, and imitate Christ in all things.

Calvin developed what he called the "third use of the law." The law, first of all, exposes sin and thus leads us to Christ through our frustration at being unable to live up to God's demands. Secondly, the law restrains injustice in society as a whole. And thirdly, the law is a guide to believers to live godly lives and should therefore be engraved on our hearts. Calvin said: "The law acts like a whip to the flesh, urging it on as men do a lazy sluggish ass."[11] It is because our Anglican Reformers adopted Calvin's view of the third use of the law that the Prayer Book instructs us to recite the Ten Commandments together out loud, both to create a sense of need for forgiveness and also that our hearts may be "inclined to keep (the) law."

The one problem with which Reformed theology has struggled down the centuries is how to apply that law to Christian behaviour without bringing back the very legalism that justification by faith leaves behind. Perhaps this is more of a psychological or spiritual problem than a theological one. Given our self-justifying natures, we always want a yardstick by which to measure our presumed improvement, and, of course, we promptly fall into the grievous sin of pride, just when we think progress has been made. We should be reminded daily of the prayer of John Newton, the converted slave trader:

> O Lord, I am not what I ought to be. Nor am I what I want to be. Nor am I what I hope to be. But I am not what I used to be, and by the grace of God I am what I am.[12]

In reply to the charge that any continued use of the law in the Christian life brings back legalism, Reformed theologians point out that sanctification is not something we do by our own effort, or even with the Spirit's help, but something that is only possible through union with Christ. Through Christ's death we are freed from the dominion of sin, and therefore, to the extent that we realize this day by day, we are set free to walk in that obedience which is "perfect freedom."

DOCTRINE AND REFORM

To say that the contemporary church must be reformed (small "r") means not only that it must acknowledge as part of its heritage these twin peaks of justification and sanctification, but also that it must continually be reformed by them. When the church forgets justification and sanctification, it does so to its peril. A glance at those periods when the church has been revitalized shows that in those periods these emphases were recovered. Augustine discovered them in the fifth century and influenced the spirituality of the church for nearly a thousand years. Luther and the other Reformers rediscovered them and reformed the church in the sixteenth century. Wesley rediscovered them again in the eighteenth century and a revival swept the English-speaking world. And one could argue that Karl Barth's commentary on Romans was essentially a rediscovery of justification in this century. Sadly, it would appear that a great many Anglicans have forgotten justification by faith and neglected the call to sanctification and holiness of life. To be vital once again and others must, by the Spirit, rediscover these key emphases of the Reformation and treasure again its reformed heritage.[13]

But the Anglican church did not merely adopt and adapt the heart of Lutheran and Calvinist reformation thinking. It made a distinct contribution all of its own. To understand this contribution, one must remember that the Anglican Reformation was less about doctrine than about politics and worship. Politically, the question was how to have a national church where the king was supreme over the pope. Liturgically, the question was how to embrace the teachings of the Reformation without cancelling out the good things which were dear to the hearts of traditional Christians.

EUCHARIST: SACRAMENT OR SACRIFICE?

Once the break with Rome was an accomplished fact, the struggle focused on the doctrine of the Eucharist or the Lord's Supper. On one side were arrayed all the Reformers who had become convinced that the Roman Catholic doctrine of transubstantiation, in which the wafer and wine actually, corporeally, and substantially became no longer bread and wine but the body and blood of Christ, was an abomination. They found it nowhere in Scripture, and they were convinced that it was bound up with the idea that the Eucharist was a propitiatory sacrifice to God rather than a sacramental meal offered to believers. Transubstantiation robbed the believer of assurance, by undercutting the "once for all" nature of the sacrifice of Christ. It robbed faith of its crucial significance by teaching that grace was infused into the recipient regardless of the state of the heart.

The primary concern of the Reformers was to ensure that the sacrament was an opportunity to draw close to the Saviour in holy communion. Therefore, it had to be approached in humility, penitence, and with a lively faith in Christ. When it was, the benefits of Christ's once-for-all sacrifice were made real and the grace of forgiveness and renewal was given. As long as the official view of the Church in England endorsed transubstantiation, these Reformers would not rest. After all, to them the entire nature of the sacrament was altered by transubstantiation from an occasion for communion with Christ into an objective external act in which Christ remained at a distance.

THE REAL PRESENCE IN COMMUNION

Did the Reformers believe in the real presence, that is, that Christ is really present when we take Holy Communion? The answer depends on what is meant by the phrase "real presence." In Cranmer's first Prayer Book, his more catholic one, only the first part of the words of administration were used: "The body of our Lord Jesus Christ which was given for thee preserve thy body and soul unto everlasting life." But in Cranmer's second Prayer Book, compiled, like the first, under Edward VI, Henry's Protestant son, only the second part was used: "Take and eat this in remembrance that Christ died for thee and feed on him in thy heart by faith with thanksgiving." It wasn't until Elizabeth's reign that the two phrases were combined as we now have them in our Prayer Book, and Anglicanism set its course to the "left" of Rome and to the "right" of the Puritans.

Cranmer and the other Reformers, with the exception of Luther, did in fact believe in the real presence, but not in a corporal or physical sense. Christ was present spiritually in the sacrament, to be received not by the mouth but by the heart. The bread and wine do not become the substance of the body and blood of Christ, but to the heart of the believer they are its sign. The Reformers had no doubt about Christ's presence. He was present to bless believers, and to judge those who ate and drank unworthily to their own damnation. With Calvin, the Anglican Reformers believed that Christ's bodily presence was in heaven, not on earth. But his spiritual presence was wherever the Church gathered in his name, and especially in the sacrament of the body and the blood. Cranmer put it this way:

> as Christ is a spiritual meat, so is He spiritually eaten and digested with the spiritual part of us, and giveth us spiritual and eternal life, and is not eaten, swallowed, and digested with our teeth, tongues, throats, and bellies.[14]

Christ's presence, then, was a sacramental presence, not a physical presence. He is in the bread the way something signified is in the sign which points to it. His body is not brought down from heaven to us, as the Roman Church taught. Rather it is we who by faith are lifted up to heaven that we might commune with him there. Consecration, then, does not effect a change in the bread and wine. Rather it changes the use to which the elements are put. It sets them apart for spiritual and godly use. Since there is no physical change in the elements, the Reformers disallowed any ceremonial actions which implied that the consecrated bread should be worshipped, adored, or held up for contemplation.

Not all Anglicans are completely happy with this. Some have wanted to move the Church in a more Roman Catholic direction. By the same token, not all Roman Catholics are happy with transubstantiation, and some today, like Catholic theologians in Holland, talk of "trans-signification", which is a lot closer to Cranmer's view. So the debate goes on.

FANATICISM OR FAITHFULNESS?

But, looking back, was it worth it? Is all the ink and blood spilled over precisely how Christ is present in the consecrated bread and wine something to be proud of? Those, of course, who are unconcerned about precisely what words are used in worship will not think so. Nor will those who come to church just to get a weekly dose of good feeling care much what it is that makes them feel good. Nor will it have been worthwhile for those who do not ground their whole salvation on the sufficiency of Christ's once-for-all sacrifice on the cross. To them, this chapter of church history was simply a period of political instability when religious fanatics split hairs over non-essentials.

I believe that, had we lived through those days, had we known what it was to try to earn our salvation through keeping the law, had we wrestled with the meaning of God's Word in search of peace for our troubled consciences, we would think differently.

LIGHTING A CANDLE

While imprisoned in the Tower of London by Queen Mary, Latimer was given an opportunity to recant and reaffirm the doctrine of transubstantiation. He declined, sealing his fate. Together with Bishop Ridley he was burned at the stake in Oxford on October 15, 1555. The precise place of their martyrdom is marked today with a stone X in the middle of a busy street. When I was a theological student there in the fifties, I used to pass it with awe.

Latimer's closing words will be remembered by all who cherish our Anglican church's reformed heritage and know their English history. Standing back to back with Ridley at the stake to which they were chained, with a bag of gunpowder around their necks to hasten death when the flames reached that high, Latimer said "Be of good comfort, Master Ridley, and play the man. We shall this day light such a candle by God's grace in England as I trust shall never be put out!"

ENDNOTES

1 Marcus L. Loane, *Masters of the English Reformation* (London: Church Book Room Press: 1954), p.94.

2 Roland H. Bainton, *The Reformation of the Sixteenth Century* (Boston: Beacon Press, 1952), p. 12, 14.

3 Bainton, Ibid, p. 8.

4 John R.H. Moorman, *A History of the Church in England* (New York, Morehouse-Barlow, 1959), pp.118-22. See also *The Oxford Dictionary of the Christian Church*, F.L.Cross ed. (London: Oxford University Press, 1958), p. 1480.

5 Galatians 2:15-21.

6 John R.W. Stott, *The Message of Galatians* (London: InterVarsity Press, 1968), p. 59.

7 Peter Toon, *Protestants and Catholics* (Ann Arbor: Servant, 1983), p. 85.

8 Hans Kung, *Justification* (London: Nelson & Sons, 1969), p. 206, 210.

9 Robert Horn, *Go Free! The Meaning of Justification* (Downers Grove: InterVarsity Press, 1976), pp. 125-6.

10 See *Evangelical Anglicans and the ARCIC Final Report: An Assessment and Critique* (second edition), ed. John Stott (Bramcote, Nottinghamshire: Grove Books, NG9 3DS, UK)

11 *Institutes*, i. p. 309.

12 Quoted in John Stott, *The Contemporary Christian* (Downers Grove: InterVarsity Press, 1992), p. 386. The saying is attributed to Newton by J.C. Ryle.

13 See Richard F. Lovelace, *Dynamics of Spiritual Life* (Downers Grove: InterVarsity Press, 1979), pp. 98-119.

14 *Works*, p.207f.

The touch of the spirit

David Watson (1933-1984) was one of the most promising younger leaders in the Church of England until his death from cancer after a year-long struggle. David transformed a derelict church adjacent to York Minster in the north of England into a dynamic missionary community that infused faith and life into people around the globe. His life and witness touched thousands through film, books, university missions, drama teams, Christian festivals, televised debates and speaking engagements. His vision of the church was undergirded by a deep biblical faith and charismatic experience. What do we have to learn from him and others who have felt the touch of the Spirit in new ways in our generation?

CHARISMATIC
The word of life and power
— ✝ ————————————————

The words that I have been using to describe the
church represent the different-coloured threads that
together make up the coat of many colours which is
the Church of Jesus Christ. Ideally, they should be
descriptive of every church. But sadly, instead of
the coat of many colours it ought to be, we find
that the typical church is more like a grey flannel
suit composed of one, or maybe two, of these
threads to the exclusion of the others.

Many churches, while comfortable with some
combination of the first three words that I have
mentioned, become distinctly uneasy when the
word "charismatic" is introduced. The word "charismatic" moves us a little further away from our
comfort zone. The reason for this is probably our
association of the word with elements of spirituality
or theology with which we disagree or which we
cannot fit into our own experience. But the word
"charismatic", rightly understood, belongs to the
whole church and should not be surrendered to a
group or movement that has self-consciously
claimed it for themselves. Any church that seeks to

be faithful to all that Jesus has revealed about his church should be charismatic.

A LUNATIC FRINGE?

It is easy to caricature the charismatic as unbalanced, extreme, and overly emotional. But caution is needed here — lest we lump what may be a genuine work of the Holy Spirit together with the ranting of extremists and even lunatics. I recall, as a teenager, standing outside the doors of a Pentecostal church on a warm Florida evening with a school roommate during spring vacation. We had stopped our car and got out to investigate what sounded like strange goings-on. As we approached the church, we could hear moaning and shouting, among other noises. "What's going on in there?" I asked a large woman who appeared to be guarding the entrance. "It all depends on what happens when the Lord gets a hold of you," she drawled. That was enough for us. Before being "got a hold of by the Lord," we disappeared down the road in a cloud of dust.

Every wing of the church universal has its lunatics. There are evangelicals with plastic smiles who alienate the very people they seek to win. There are Catholics who should have been born in the Dark Ages. Some reformed folk are so acerbic that they sound like they have been baptized in lemon juice. Similarly, some charismatics are so focused on dramatic signs, so prone to excessive emotion, so reeking of spiritual superiority, and so anti-intellectual in their faith that they appear, like cult devotees, to be victims of mob psychology. One looks in vain for theological balance, spiritual maturity, and social concern. But it is foolish as well as unfair to lump all charismatics together and reject an entire wing of the worldwide church on the basis of its extremist elements.

There is clearly a difference between the modern charismatic culture and the charisms which St. Paul sees to be a normal part of New Testament church life. The modern charismatic movement confuses the biblical bestowal of grace gifts, which has its roots in the Greek word charis (grace), with the natural endowments of certain personalities recognized as having "charisma," that is the power to attract and compel others. Biblically, the receiving of grace is the indispensable mark of a Christian, and without it no one is a Christian at all.[1] And the apostolic teaching is that once that grace has been received, unique gifts are given to enable the Christian to participate in the strengthening and upbuilding of the body of Christ. These gifts can range from the extremely mundane (administration, hospitality, teaching) to the very dramatic (tongues, interpretation, prophecy, miracles).[2] The charismatic culture strays from the biblical vision when it lavishes attention on the more dramatic gifts and ignores all the other gifts which have been responsible for the church's growth and effectiveness through the ages.

Biblically, the emphasis is on the Giver rather than the gift. The charismatic culture, unfortunately, reverses this emphasis by its pursuit of "charisma" rather than "charism." When these two qualities coexist in the same person, the untaught confuse the two without realizing it and honor either the wrong person — or the right person for the wrong reasons. Charisma can be possessed by good and bad leaders alike and has led many astray. No wonder the public at large seems unimpressed by the shouts, grunts, saccharine smiles and smooth rhetoric of tel-evangelists and instead questions the integrity of their motives. What matters for the work of Christ is the charism, not the charisma.

Beyond the dangerous exaltation of personality there remain other valid criticisms of the charismatic culture. There is its unconvincing biblical exegesis, in which passages are twisted to justify the idea that a second blessing must occur after one's conversion to Christ. There is its triumphalist emphasis on power and victory, to the neglect of honesty and penitence. And there is its narrow concern for personal morals coupled with a failure to face the reality of corporate and systemic evil — especially in regions like Latin America. But when all this has been said, we must ask the sobering question of whether, if we confine our investigation to merely voicing these criticisms, we have done justice to the breadth of biblical teaching on the Holy Spirit and his gifts and to the experience of hundreds of millions of Christians around the world who claim to have found the reality of a deeper dimension to their faith through the Holy Spirit.

ORIGINS AND GROWTH IN MODERN TIMES

While claiming antecedents throughout the history of the church, the modern recovery of charismatic experience can be traced to late 19th century America where a series of events led to an outbreak of "speaking in tongues" at an extended series of revival meetings on Azuza Street in Los Angeles in April of 1906. Despite such humble, some would even say zany, beginnings, the phenomenon known as Pentecostalism has grown in the past nine decades to encompass approximately 333 million Christians worldwide. Together, charismatics and Pentecostals are the fastest-growing Christian movement in the world. They create new churches. They are present in nearly all Christian denominations, including the Roman Catholic Church. There are charismatics among bishops, clergy, monks and nuns. Recent studies estimate that at least 18% of all North American Anglicans are charismatic. Most of these are lifelong Anglicans. At least half of them tithe. A majority are involved in their parish and feel a loyalty to their denomination.

Just as there are similarities between evangelicals and Fundamentalists, so there are similarities between charismatics and Pentecostals. But the differences are also noteworthy. One writer puts the differences this way:

> Pentecostalism arose early in the first half of this century, charismatics in the second half. Pentecostals formed the classical Pentecostal denominations; charismatics remained in their own (mainstream) churches. Most ... Pentecostals insist on (speaking in) tongues as (the) initial evidence (of baptism in the Holy Spirit); charismatics generally speak in tongues but do not make it a matter of necessity. Pentecostals teach a strict subsequence of vital Christian experiences ... Charismatics ... find ways to fit charismatic experience and renewal into their existing ecclesiastical and theological traditions. Pentecostals, at least the North American varieties, are likely to reflect the rigoristic mores rising from their holiness origins and fundamentalist encounter; charismatics might smoke pipes or attend dances, depending on their church customs. (In worship) Pentecostals (tend to) raise their arms fully over-

head, palms forward, (while) charismatics ... extend palms up, elbows bent at the waist.[3]

But much of this is mere sociological analysis which, if void of theological reflection, encourages the attitude that charismatic experience can be dismissed as the sign of some troubling neurosis that is afflicting religious folk in this age of uncertainty. But we ought not to be content to leave the whole subject on a sociological basis, allowing criteria which are essentially cultural and emotional to dictate our response. We should never permit serious theological issues to be judged on the basis of taste, musical sophistication, emotional style, cultural preference, and psychological compatibility. To allow our judgement to be so clouded is to blind ourselves to the church's inglorious tradition of suppressing prophets, resisting truth, and quenching the Spirit — and perhaps even risk adding to that tradition. There is a frightening irony in the words of Gamaliel to the Sanhedrin: "If this is of men, it will fail; but if it is of God; you will not be able to overthrow it. You might even be found opposing God!"[4]

REDEFINING THE TERM *CHARISMATIC*

A glance at the following text offers us a window through which to watch the young church in action, and it offers insights which help us towards a redefinition of the word "charismatic." What we see in this passage is a church operating under the control and direction of the Holy Spirit:

100

Now those who were scattered because of the persecution that arose over Stephen traveled as far as Phoenicia and Cyprus and Antioch, speaking the word to none except Jews. But there were some of them, men of Cyprus and Cyrene, who on coming to Antioch spoke to the Greeks also, preaching the Lord Jesus. And the hand of the Lord was with them, and a great number that believed turned to the Lord. News of this came to the ears of the church in Jerusalem, and they sent Barnabas to Antioch. When he came and saw the grace of God, he was glad; and he exhorted them all to remain faithful to the Lord with steadfast purpose; for he was a good man, full of the Holy Spirit and of faith. And a large company was added to the Lord. So Barnabas went to Tarsus to look for Saul; and when he had found him, he brought him to Antioch. For a whole year they met with the church, and taught a large company of people; and in Antioch the disciples were for the first time called Christians. [5]

Jesus promised that the Spirit he would send would bring new life. Like the wind that blows this way and that, we would see its effects, even if we could not understand its origin. Is this why, when Barnabas arrived in Antioch, he was able to *see* the grace of God? Luke tells us that the "hand of the Lord was with" the men of Cyprus and Cyrene — apparently a code phrase for the manifestation of signs and wonders accompanying the preaching of the Gospel. Luke wants his readers to understand that the accep-

tance of the Gospel by these Greek-speaking Anti-
ochans was evidenced by visible signs of the kingdom's arrival — healings, deliverances, lives
dramatically turned from idolatry and sorcery, and
much rejoicing.

Secondly, Luke clearly indicates that it was the
preaching of the Lord Jesus — or of Jesus as Lord
— that converted the people of Antioch. By this a
true convert was to be known. They were able to
confess Jesus as Lord, and they sought to live lives
in concert with that confession. So to ensure the
faithfulness of these converts, they were given a full
year of teaching under the authority of Barnabas and
Paul. Here, then, is a church that takes seriously
the Word of God, that is learning to judge all
things by the apostolic testimony to God's Word.

The importance of teaching was underscored by
Jesus who promised that the Spirit he would send
would lead his followers into all truth. Because the
Holy Spirit is the Spirit of truth, the ability to recognize truth from falsehood is to be one of the
marks of the Spirit-led disciples.[6] In a similar vein,
St. Paul says that no matter how apparently moved
by the Spirit someone may be, the church is to
recognize those who have the Holy Spirit by their
confession that Jesus is Lord. Hence what they say
about Jesus is to be the telltale sign of whether they
really have the Spirit or not.[7]

Thirdly, as Jesus identified the Spirit with love and St. Paul says that to have the Spirit within is to know the love of Christ and to have it shed abroad in our hearts[8], the supreme mark of the presence of Christ in any church is love that is shown in practical ways. So, reading this passage from Acts 11, I am drawn to consider the character of the man who is sent from Jerusalem to Antioch. Barnabas is known for his generosity and encouragement.[9] This indicates to me that the first response of the Jerusalem Church to these new converts was to welcome them as fellow Christians. Notice also that the believers were a recognizable community in Antioch, sufficiently identified as to have been given a nickname, Christians. Would this community of Jews and Gentiles have received that name had they not publicly demonstrated a particular love for each other which was capable of transcending the age-old divide between Jew and non-Jew? A merely sentimental love would not have sufficed. And then, after Agabus prophesied a coming famine, was it sentiment that these new believers sent south? No, it was relief.

Finally, recalling Jesus' promise that the Spirit would empower them to witness, convict the world of sin and righteousness and judgment, and to glorify him through their personal testimony, I note the sense of mission which breathes through the entire book of Acts and is expressed in this mission to

Antioch. Here a small interracial band of men, probably including (according to Acts 13:1) Simeon Niger (who was black) and Lucius of Cyrene, are called to leave family and employment behind, in order to preach the good news. The result is a remarkable response to the gospel among non-Jews in a city known for its paganism and immorality. As so often appears to be the case, one of the marks of the Spirit's presence is witness which effectively penetrates the traditional structures of society. No doubt the presence of a team of witnesses united by a common loyalty to Christ across the barriers of race and culture greatly enhanced the power of their preaching.

FOUR KEY CHARACTERISTICS

Here are four characteristics, then, which together mark the New Testament church as charismatic. Moreover, they give us all-important clues as to what should constitute the meaning of "charismatic" for the church today:

• **Life.** The church is not just activity and bustle and programs. It is the life of the Holy Spirit manifested in people who, newly born into the kingdom, demonstrate that new life in ways that show the power of God.

As Donald Bloesch writes:

> The gifts of the Holy Spirit will be in evidence not only in the pulpit but in Sunday school classes, youth groups,

and prayer and Bible study groups. The laity will be the missionary arm of the church, for it is through their outreach in the community that the spiritually lost will hear the good news and will be brought into the worship and life of the church.[10]

In a charismatic church, one will find people who have been delivered from addictions, saved from hopelessness and despair, healed in body and in spirit, reconciled across social and cultural divisions, and who because of their unashamed testimony to these blessings are joyful in worship.

• **Truth.** In a charismatic church there will be no merely pedantic concern for doctrine or theology. Rather, one will find a wholehearted loyalty to all that has been revealed to us through the witness of the Apostles. A charismatic church will uplift Jesus as Lord without self-consciousness. There, both preaching and teaching will be honored as they obviously were in Antioch. And there one will find people who are full of the Holy Spirit and full of faith — like Barnabas.

• **Love.** A charismatic church will evidence a love that transcends differences. It will not be just a friendly church where bonhomie passes for real fellowship. It will be a church where different classes, races, and sexes come together in a love that is fleshed out in sacrificial caring for one another. It is a church where people's hearts are sometimes painfully open to each other. As the Prior of Taizé once wrote: "To have opted for love is a choice which opens a wound from which one never recovers."[11]

• **Mission.** Since all the New Testament writers connect the coming of the Spirit with mission, any claimed experience of the Spirit which does not result in missionary and evangelistic work of some sort ought to be suspect. Since the reason for the gifts of the Spirit is the upbuilding of the body of Christ, in a charismatic church, all will be concerned in one way or another to see the church grow in numbers and depth.

WARINESS OR WELCOME

Unfortunately, while the churches pay lip service to these qualities, they have not always welcomed them. Consequently, the word "charismatic" has been relegated to a movement rather than owned by the whole church. For example, the Presiding Bishop of the Episcopal Church warns against a resurgence of "biblicism", and thereby reveals the institutional church's lack of ease with those aspects of renewal which it cannot control.[12]

However, not all church leaders have resisted what God is doing. Cardinal Suenens of Belgium welcomed the charismatic phenomenon, saying:

> The Church has never known a more critical moment in her history. From a human point of view, there is no

help on the horizon. We do not see from where salvation can come unless from Him; there is no salvation, except in his name. [Yet] at this moment, we see in the sky of the Church the manifestations of the Holy Spirit's action which seem to be like those known to the early Church. It is as though the Acts of the Apostles and the letters of St. Paul were coming to life again, as if God were once more breaking into our history.[13]

Churchgoers who resist the genuine manifestations of the Spirit must share the blame for turning the charismatic dimension of our common Christian life into a separate movement with excesses, imbalances, and a free rein for the lunatic fringe. It is these excesses and imbalances which cry out for the comprehensive ministry of the whole church. Just as the cults are the "unpaid debts" of the church, so the charismatic movement draws attention to a long-neglected dimension of Christian experience which ought to be at the center of every church's life. As James Dunn says, "Pentecostal teaching on spiritual gifts, including glossolalia, while still unbalanced, is much more soundly based on the NT than is generally recognized."[14]

DANGERS TO AVOID

However, three dangers need to be faced and dealt with. First, the charismatic movement so stresses personal experience that it can encourage an unhealthy individualism. Some seek specific gifts more from a desire for personal enhancement than for the good of the body. Gifted individuals become laws unto themselves with no accountability to the structures of a local Christian community.

Secondly, I sense that too many in the charismatic movement bypass Good Friday in their haste to experience Easter and Pentecost. For example, I hear little from the charismatic movement about sin, struggle, the need to mortify the flesh, the need to die daily to oneself, and the sanctifying use of suffering. The impression is frequently given that, by means of one overwhelming experience, we can rise above these things and experience victory, power, and joy. In view of this tendency, we should recall that, because Paul so clearly saw this danger in Corinth, he downplayed his own spiritual experiences, and gloried in his weaknesses and the sufficiency of God's grace. It is the nature of the flesh to want to "appear" strong; whereas true strength is found in bearing with weaknesses in such a way that God's power is revealed.[15]

Thirdly, I fear that the charismatic movement may be in danger of institutionalizing the Spirit — that is, of creating forms and structures to contain the new life, forms which then must be perpetuated long after they have become outmoded and need to die. For example, the so-called shepherding movement went overboard in seeking to help people gain mastery over sin by coming under the authority of another. Also, the reliance on certain techniques to whip up enthusiasm at meetings, the formula approach to healing, the "name it and claim it" approach to prayer, and perhaps even the "unanimity principle" applied to decision-making may each have once served a purpose. But they should not be institutionalized permanently. We must always ask what new skins are needed to hold the new wine of the Spirit.

LESSONS TO LEARN

These criticisms of excesses in the charismatic movement must not blind us to the lessons that the church as a whole needs to learn. Charismatics on the whole know more about spiritual warfare than most Christians. They have faced the darkness in themselves in a more realistic way than many of us have. They have learned to appropriate the armor of God in confronting evil. No one would argue that every problem has a demon behind it. But we have much to be taught about deliverance, boldness in prayer, and even exorcism.

Charismatics have rediscovered the material order in worship. They are unafraid of touching, hugging, raising hands, dancing, drama and color. They lay hands on one another for healing, blessing, and the infilling of the Spirit. Is this not an extension of the principle of the incarnation, that God became flesh? Is the self-consciousness with which many Christians approach worship really of God? Part of the liberty which the Spirit gives is the freedom to express faith and joy in outwardly sacramental ways.

Charismatics expect God to heal more often than many Christians do. Why should this time-honored dimension of the Church's witness be left in the hands of those on the fringe? While recognizing the dangers, should we not pray more fervently for God to intervene through and beyond modern medicine, as he often has done in the past?

Charismatics expect the presence of the gifts of the Spirit and give time in worship for their use. Donald Coggan, Archbishop of Canterbury, once asked: "Why is it that the Pentecostal Churches are growing at such a phenomenal rate? Is it possible that they have the gifts of the Spirit which we have not?"[16] Gifts come in many packages; but they need to be opened and used. The emphasis in the New Testament is not on seeking the gifts of the Spirit, but rather on using those which we have been given. Naturally, we need to discover our gifts by trial and error. But more important, we need to create a climate in which gifts are welcomed and used. I do not believe that gifts like tongues and prophecy are normally meant to be used in the main services of worship. I agree with Donald Bloesch who says that they normally belong in special meetings or semi-private gatherings where they can be tested in the light of Scripture before being publicized. But we should not inhibit them nor be inhibited by them.

AN OUTSTANDING EXAMPLE

David Watson is the man with whom I most closely identify the positive values of the charismatic movement. Of the six "heroes" profiled in this book, he is the only one who lived in the twentieth century and whom I actually knew. Our paths crossed on several occasions.

David was the son of a military officer who had refused medical help because he was a Christian Scientist. He died when David was ten, leaving him both skeptical and curious about spiritual things. David dabbled with spiritualism and Buddhism, and then opted for atheism until, during his freshman year at Cambridge, he was converted. After his conversion he was immensely fortunate to have David Sheppherd, one of England's most famous cricketers and the future Bishop of Liverpool, as his spiritual guide. Under Sheppherd's tutelage, Watson was soon demonstrating qualities of character and faith that indicated that he was developing into an outstanding Christian leader.

After serving two curacies, David took over St. Cuthbert's, a derelict church adjacent to York Minster, the huge cathedral in the North of England.

From almost nothing, under his leadership over a 17-year period, there arose a large community of faith which was to draw visitors from around the world. Aside from his regular parish duties and many public appearances, he participated in more than 60 university missions alone! David always uplifted Jesus as Lord in a way that enabled people from all walks of life to come to faith and to be incorporated into lively, growing fellowships.

FEAR NO EVIL

And then it happened. He received a diagnosis of cancer. A hasty operation revealed that the cancer had spread from the colon to the liver, and, in a matter of a few brief days, David was given a sentence of death. The world prayed and hundreds came to his bedside, including the Archbishops of both Canterbury and York. Many times, he was encouraged to claim total healing, even though carcinoma of the liver is invariably fatal. There were remissions, only to be followed by serious relapses. As the months wore one, David wrote his last book, entitled *Fear No Evil*[17], about his struggle with cancer. On February 18, 1984, David Watson died peacefully in his bed.

David is my model charismatic for two reasons, first because of his undeniably Spirit-filled ministry, which I touched on above, and second because of his surprising Spirit-led honesty. David was remarkably honest about his suffering. He hated pain. He was frightened, he doubted God, and he cried. He recorded his weakness and fear quite straightforwardly, and yet with an underlying trust in the Lord that has made his experience a comfort to thousands who have walked the same lonesome valley as he. It is impossible to come away from reading *Fear No Evil* without feeling that this man knew God.

David was similarly honest about his theology. Although very drawn to the typical two-stage theology common among Pentecostals and charismatics, David was too grounded in biblical theology to go along with it. His studies had led him to see that faith, forgiveness, justification, baptism, and the gifts of the Spirit all rightly belong to Christian initiation — that is, they are a cluster of things, all of which coinhere in our initial coming to Christ. Nevertheless, David observed that they are not all experienced simultaneously. The experience of being overwhelmed by the love of God, when the Spirit is poured out upon us, may come later, even though, in principle, when we come to Christ the Spirit is ours. David refused to teach a two-stage experience as normative for everyone. He even disavowed the use of the phrase "baptism in the Holy Spirit" to describe a second experience because he would not separate what God had joined together.[18] But that did not keep him from wanting every church and every individual to remain open to the constant need of being filled with the Spirit.

A SOLID CORE WITH SOFT EDGES

I hope that the legacy of the modern resurgence of charismatic experience will be a church that, as a whole, is challenged to a new openness to the Holy Spirit. As Sam Shoemaker once said, the real "lunatic fringe" today may not be the people we call the "crackpots", but rather all of us who, though in the churches, are out of the Spirit.[19]

To be in the Spirit does not imply that we embrace some generic "spirituality" such as mysticism, earth-ism, feminism, or Jungian psychology (though we may have insights to learn from each of these fashions of thought). It is primarily to be in Christ, in the sense that the good news of his love has become the center of our lives.

Only when our lives have this solid core can they afford to have the soft edges that enable people to get close and the church to become the loving fellowship it professes to be. When the core of our lives is not strong, our edges tend to get rough and people keep their distance.

1 Rom. 5:1,2; Eph.2:8,9.

2 Rom. 12:6-8; I Cor. 12:1-14:39; I Pet. 4:10.

3 Russell P. Spitler, "Pentecostal Spirituality" in *Christian Spirituality: Five Views of Sanctification*, ed Donald L. Alexander (Downers Grove: InterVarsity Press, 1988), p. 134-153.

4 Acts. 5:38,39.

5 Acts 11:19-30.

6 Jn. 16:13; 15:26; 14:26.

7 I Cor. 12:3; Jn. 17:26; Eph. 3:19; Rom. 5:5.

8 Jn. 15:26; 16:13; I Cor. 12:2,3.

9 Because of his magnanimity of spirit and his practical application of gospel truth, a Canadian fellowship of evangelical Anglican clergy and laity has named itself Barnabas Anglican Ministries.

10 *Essentials of Evangelical Theology*, Vol.2 (New York: Harper & Row, 1979), p. 123.

11 Quoted in *I Believe in the Church*, David Watson (Grand Rapids: Eerdmans, 1978) p. 366.

12 *New Millenium, New Church*, Richard Kew, Roger J. White (Cambridge: Cowley, 1992), p. 20.

13 *A New Pentecost?*, Leon J. Suenens (New York: Seabury, 1975), p. 90.

14 *Baptism in the Holy Spirit*, James D.G. Dunn (London: SCM, 1970), p. 229.

15 *A Theology of the Holy Spirit*, Frederick Dale Bruner (Grand Rapids: Eerdmans, 1970), pp. 285-319. This chapter has been one of the most formative influences in my understanding of the spiritual life.

16 Watson, op. cit. p.256.

17 London: Hodder & Stoughton, 1984.

18 I Cor. 12:13.

19 *With the Holy Spirit and with Fire*, Samuel M. Shoemaker
  (New York: Harper & Row, 1960), p. 52.

118

Christ's call upon life

Phillips Brooks (1834-1893) was a towering
figure, both physically and spiritually, in the
American Church in the latter half of the last
century. First in Philadelphia and then while he
was Rector of Trinity Church, Boston, his sermons drew wide attention, first when preached
and later when published. His Lectures on
Preaching were standard reading in seminaries
across the land for decades, and his Christmas
carol "O Little Town of Bethlehem" is beloved
everywhere. What attracted people to this bach-
elor clergyman? Why did his expression of
Christianity touch such a deep chord in nineteenth century America? How can his liberality
of spirit teach us something about the church of
Jesus Christ?

LIBERAL
The word of love
and openness
— ✠ —————————————————————

IT IS UNFORTUNATE that the words "conservative" and "liberal" have always been politicized, and hence polarized. But in the past, say a hundred years ago during the days of Phillips Brooks, they were thought to have different meanings in different contexts. One could be conservative in some areas of thought and liberal in others, as we shall see was the case with Phillips Brooks. However, today the use of these two loaded words in politics is thought to govern their use in other areas.

However, the lines are not always as neatly drawn as some would have us believe. And people do switch their allegiances depending upon their circumstances. For example, a conservative can be a liberal who has just been mugged; while a liberal can be a conservative who has just been arrested! Neoconservatives can be "liberals with daughters in high school" while neoliberals can be conservatives with a child who has just joined a cult.

It is easy for the church to get caught in the crossfire between these two camps. Nor is the matter helped by the fact that many Christians seem happy to simply identify themselves with one label or the other. When this happens, churches begin to divide along ideological lines and communication becomes extremely difficult. Rather than dialogue between different camps one encounters "two solitudes."

Clearly, the church must conserve what is good in the past. Such a role seems implied by the first four words I have used to describe the church: Evangelical conserves the evangel, the Gospel. Catholic conserves the catholic faith enshrined in the Creeds. Reformed conserves the great themes of the Reformation; and charismatic, while not conservative in form, certainly is conservative in the sense that the Holy Spirit witnesses to the enduring truth of Jesus Christ. Indeed, in Roman Catholic circles, charismatics are among the most traditional in doctrine, in acceptance of religious authority, and on moral issues.

ETHOS AND THEOLOGY

But those who quite rightly see the church as a conserving force should not easily dispense with the word "liberal" simply because of its association with political or cultural trends with which they may not agree. They must see that we can use words like "liberal" and "conservative" about the church in two fundamentally different ways. They can refer either to the ethos of a church or to its theology. Consequently, at least four permutations are possible: a church can be conservative in ethos but liberal in theology; or a church can be liberal in ethos, but conservative in theology. Or a church can be conservative both in ethos and theology, or liberal both in ethos and theology.

To illustrate this, suppose for a moment that you have just joined a thoroughly conservative church — one that is conservative both in ethos and theology. I suspect that you will begin to notice several of the following characteristics:

A fortress mentality will pervade the thinking of the membership. Nothing is said openly, of course. But you pick up an impression that the congregation sees itself as manning the ramparts against invaders eager to do away with all that is good in the past, which, you come to realize after a while, is synonymous with all that is good. There is a lack of diversity in expression or thinking on theological, cultural, or social issues. Disagreement is discouraged or possibly even suppressed by those in authority. A judgemental spirit towards other Christian bodies, sometimes amounting to a rejection of the validity of their churches' ministries, might prevail as well.

There are unspoken alliances with non-religious groups that are self-consciously conservative or even reactionary, for example, political groups on the far right, ethnic groups dedicated to continuing a linguistic or cultural heritage, or social groups like the landed gentry, or para-religious groups like the Masons or the Knights of Columbus, and even, in extreme cases, racist groups. You would discover narrow views on nonessentials. For instance, if the church is a conservative catholic one, issues of gesture, vesture, and posture seem very important — at least to the clergy. But if the church is a conservative protestant one, then taboos about social, cultural, and recreational activities define the parameters of holiness. You probably pick up a hostile attitude towards the creative arts and an uninformed suspicion of secular knowledge. You likely find that troublesome questions of biblical interpretation are brushed aside or given inadequate stock answers.

ATTITUDES

You might notice other typically conservative attitudes. Families that do not fit the nuclear model are ever-so-subtly relegated to second-class citizenship, along with singles. Women are excluded from leadership positions, such as the governing board or the vestry (as well as, of course, the ordained ministry) — on doctrinal grounds. When the will of God is brought up, it is generally presented as the opposite of one's own will. Spiritual blessings are understood as gained primarily at the expense of worldly pleasures. Any who falls into grievous sin after making a

Christian profession is viewed as almost certainly unredeemable.

Moreover, if you question any of these unspoken attitudes, you will be told, assuming that the congregation is growing in numbers, that the numerical growth is God's seal of approval upon their attitudes and behaviour. In the event that the membership happens to be stagnant or declining, you will be informed that the elect are always a faithful few! Echoes of this cultural conservatism are found in Lytton Strachey's colorful description of English church life in the early nineteenth century, when cultural conservatism combined comfortably with pastoral laziness:

> Portly divines subscribed with a sigh or a smile to the Thirty-Nine Articles, sank quietly into easy livings, rode gaily to hounds of a morning as gentlemen should, and, as gentlemen should, carried their two bottles of an evening ... The fervours of piety, the zeal of Apostolic charity, the enthusiasm of self-renunciation — these things were all very well in their way and in their place; but their place was certainly not in the Church of England ... The great bulk of the clergy walked calmly along the smooth road of ordinary duty. They kept an eye on the poor of the parish, and they conducted the Sunday Services in a becoming manner; for the rest, they differed neither outwardly nor inwardly from the

great bulk of the laity, to whom the Church was a
useful organisation for the maintenance of Religion, as
by law established.[1]

One is reminded of Samuel Butler's critique of the
same period of English church life. "They would
have been equally horrified at hearing the Christian
religion doubted, and at seeing it practiced."[2]

Cultural conservatism and responsible theological
conservatism are two quite different things. When
Dean M. Kelley wrote *Why Conservative Churches are
Growing* in 1977, he defined conservative churches as
those which are strong on meaning — that is, they
seek to give biblical answers to life's questions.
They are also strong on expectations — that is,
they call for a high level of commitment in time,
talent, and treasure. And they are strong on accountability — they expect conformity in moral behaviour. Given this definition, it is quite possible to
be conservative and yet to have very few of the
characteristics mentioned above. In fact, Kelley —
not a theological conservative himself — found
those churches that are merely conservative in ethos
to be not conservative enough. The self-consciously
conservative church, he said, is often straining to
preserve the more familiar and lesser attachments of
a generation ago, while neglecting the more pro-
found and enduring goods from the distant past.

This is why prophets are always necessary. Prophets criticize what is newly sacrosanct, and call people back to earlier and more fundamental truths.[3]

It is important, therefore, to keep separate in one's mind ethos (local cultural beliefs and behaviour) and theology. Many churches that are liberal in theology are remarkably conservative in ethos. For example, the Virgin Birth may be doubted from the pulpit without provoking any lay comment at all, but the introduction of a minor liturgical change or the suggestion that sherry might be offered along with coffee after church can cause pandemonium.

LIBERAL THEOLOGY

Liberal theology, as opposed to liberal politics and culture, arose in the nineteenth century, principally in Germany, as an adaptation of eighteenth century Enlightenment principles to the field of religion. Scholars began to say that, since all biblical interpreters of the past were governed by creedal and theological biases, they could never give us a true historical view of the Bible. Therefore, if one were to approach the Bible scientifically and historically, one must lay aside all doctrinal bias. Liberalism, under the influence of rationalism, also said that miracles had never happened and that there were no divinely revealed truths which were to be taken on faith. The result of this was a complete change in the focus of theology. The real subject matter of theology ceased to be God and became instead the religious experiences of men and women who have believed. The Bible was not to be regarded as a revelation from God. Rather it is the record of people's religious experiences, and must be subjected to the same radical historical criticism as any other book.

Borrowing from science the idea that all life forms are evolving from lower and cruder forms to higher and more sophisticated ones, liberal theology assumed that religion experiences a similar evolution. Hence a concept or story that appears in Genesis or Leviticus must be primitive, and even a passage in St. Paul, though a great advancement on what had gone before, was still much too crude for the enlightened minds of the day. Religion's only hope, in the opinion of the theological liberal, lay in a reshaped theology and a recast morality that could fit the needs of an enlightened age. Those who opposed this patently obvious agenda were considered to be obscurantist and reactionary.

Thus liberal theology, with boundless confidence in the adequacy of human reason, is nearly always presented as eminently sensible. However, in the minds of many, it fails to qualify as Christianity at all. As J.I.Packer writes, "Liberalism is subjectivism trying to be Christianity."[4]

There is nothing quite as devastating as the criticisms of an ex-devotee. Just as Augustine's appraisal of his worldly life in the Confessions is relentlessly negative, similarly, the critique of liberal theology by Eta Linnemann will not be welcomed by her old colleagues in the prestigious Society for New Testament Studies, or her former faculty mates in the New Testament department at Marburg. But this former student of Bultmann, Fuchs, Gogarten and Ebeling, who now professes a full-blown evangelical faith replete with a high confidence in the unity and reliability of Scripture, has astounded the scholarly world by writing an impassioned call to repentance for the way modern biblical studies have been held captive to secular critical historiography. As an example of the liberal theology she now criticizes, Linnemann writes:

> That Jesus is God's Son ... is often not taken to mean that he is "God of God, Light of Light, Very God of Very God." It is understood as just a cipher which expresses that there was something special about the "historical Jesus" which sets him apart from other great figures in history, and that in him we are — somehow — in contact with God. In this connection one hears the expression that every age has its own fate and must work out its own Christology. I have heard this formula for the last thirty years. I used to propagate it myself and with great fervor waited for such a Christology — in vain. It turned out that this formula was just a charter that allowed what God's Word tells us about our Lord and

Savior Jesus to be set aside as nonbinding, as the Christology of the past.[5]

Linnemann prefaces her book by saying that she threw out all her previous theological writings upon her conversion, and she urges her readers to discard them as well. For a more irenic criticism of liberalism, and probably therefore a more useful one, I recommend Thomas Oden of Drew University. Self-styled as a repentant liberal who is now a classical Christian, Oden writes that liberal theology has been driven by a deep yearning to find some convenient means of getting itself legitimated in the eyes of modernity.[6]

RADICALISM

Many make the mistake of confusing liberal theology with radical theology. Radicalism is a wholesale and unashamed recasting of Christian belief to fit in with one of the prevailing paradigms of modern culture: feminism, earth-ism, socialism, or relativism are a few examples. An example of radical theology would be the feminization of God and the rejection of God's transcendence for a vision of God's immanence in and through the primal (feminine) forces of nature. To Rosemary Ruether, Jesus is the bearer of a liberating message that "aims at a new reality in which hierarchy and dominance are overcome as principles of social relations."[7] Radical theology got its start when Western society began to fragment into interest groups; it seems to be an attempt to "market" an ersatz Christianity to these special interests. The issue radicalism raises for the serious Christian is not whether Christianity better fits the Marxist, feminist, or earth-ist model, but whether culture is to be permitted to sit in judgment on Christian revelation, or vice versa. Radical theology is actually critical of liberal theology for its rationalism and for its idealism. But like liberalism, radicalism preempts the place of objective revelation by substituting one's own assessment of one's personal experience as its final authority.

Not all of liberalism's legacy is negative. Open-minded people will recognize its positive contributions to the church. Liberal theology has forced classical Christians to come to terms with many of the questions of the modern age, and has challenged the whole church to address itself with greater relevance to its social and cultural context. In addition, responsible (as opposed to romantic) liberalism in the 19th century must be credited with helping the church to read the Bible afresh as an historical document. I am thinking particularly of British scholars such as J.B. Lightfoot, B.F. Wescott, and F.J.A. Hort. However, those of us who were schooled in liberal theology know its deficiencies. As a system, it is useless as a tool for building the church or making the essentials of the Christian faith credible to the very modernity its advocates are so eager to impress. Liberal theology is, in fact, a dead end, as the "Death of God" movement showed in the Sixties.

THE LIBERAL ETHOS

Since the church must incarnate itself in every generation and every culture, even while it preserves the faith "once for all delivered to the saints", it needs a model of how it can be both liberal in ethos and conservative in theology. Such a model, I believe, is given us in the New Testament, and may be found in germ in Jesus' own treatment of the woman taken in adultery.

> Early in the morning he came again to the temple; all the people came to him, and he sat down and taught them. The scribes and Pharisees brought a woman who had been caught in adultery, and placing her in the midst they said to him, "Teacher, this woman has been caught in the act of adultery. Now in the law Moses commanded us to stone such. What do you say about her?" This they said to test him, that they might have some charge to bring against him. Jesus bent down and wrote with his finger on the ground. And as they continued to ask him, he stood up and said to them, "Let him who is without sin among you be the first to throw a stone at

her." And once more he bent down and wrote with his finger on the ground. But when they heard it, they went away, one by one, beginning with the eldest, and Jesus was left alone with the woman standing before him. Jesus looked up and said to her, "Woman, where are they? Has no one condemned you?" She said, "No one, Lord." And Jesus said, "Neither do I condemn you; go and do not sin again."[8]

LAW AND GOSPEL

In this passage, Jesus forbids us to read the Old Testament as a document that is complete in itself. Its completeness is only to be found when fulfilled in him. The Old Testament must not be directly applied by these men who caught the woman in adultery without being filtered through the forgiving love of Christ which is the hallmark of the kingdom of God. There can be no stoning of adulterers, because it is out of character with the culminating revelation of the Gospel. Therefore, however the original ruling may have been applied (or remitted), on account of the Gospel, Christians are not to treat people this way.

Contrast this with the case of two Muslim pilgrims returning from Mecca in 1957. They were found *in flagrante*, guilty of adultery, and were immediately sentenced to death by stoning. The two were executed the very next day, with the judge himself (the Mufti) casting the first stone! Nor was this an isolated example.[9]

One cannot help but be struck by how merciful Jesus was to the fallen woman. Without condoning her behaviour, he treated her with respect and sensitivity, refusing to fall into the legalism of her accusers. Moreover, he went beyond mercy by tipping the balance of the scales in favor of the underprivileged sex by asking the woman's accusers to pick up stones only if they were themselves without sin in this area. He knew that, whatever their outward behaviour, none of the men there would qualify as guiltless of every sexual sin. Had the Pharisees failed to bring the adulterous *man* to Jesus because they knew all too well that "boys will be boys"?

Jesus also displays remarkable wisdom. The dilemma he faced was how to avoid coming down on either side, since neither represented what he was trying to say and do. To side with the accusers would put in jeopardy his understanding of the deeper meaning of the law — that mercy triumphs over justice. To side with the woman would put him in opposition to the Law of Moses. Between a rock and a hard place, Jesus found a way through. In the silence which he gained by writing in the sand, he garnered the needed time to shift the discussion away from the breaking of a specific law to the nature of sin. Is sin only in the act, or is it also in the attitude? By probing the deeper dimensions of sin, Jesus touched the men's consciences and forced them to reflect on their own complicity in the very sin they condemned in the woman.

Finally, Jesus demonstrated a high level of faith in the woman's capacity to change. He refused to stereotype her as just an adulteress, but saw her as capable of moral transformation. With his non-condemning approach, he sent her off to lead a new life.

With this story as a background, consider the following characteristics that you should expect to find in a church that is conservative in theology, but liberal in ethos.

STILL SINNERS

A liberal church is a forgiving church. It is a church where, as Luther put it, people are *simul justus et peccator* — a Latin phrase meaning that people are both justified, and yet remain sinners. In a forgiving church, people do not have to hide the fact that they are sinners. "The pious fellowship," said Bonhoeffer, "permits no one to be a sinner. So everybody must conceal his sin from himself and from the fellowship. We dare not be sinners. Many Christians are unthinkably horrified when a real sinner is suddenly discovered among the righteous. So we remain in our sin, living in lies and hypocrisy."[10] Churches that are conservative in ethos are too eager to separate the wheat from the chaff here and now. They forget that Jesus told us specifically to await the separation that will occur on the day of God's judgment.[11]

A liberal church is a gender-neutral church. It resists changing God from Father to Mother for many reasons, including the simple fact that the God Jesus called "Father" is a far cry from the patriarchal monster feminists excoriate. But a church with a liberal ethos recognizes that women have often been shortchanged in our culture and are frequently not treated as full partners along with men. Therefore, a liberal church resists those subtle forms of discrimination against women that pass as acceptable in conservative churches. The church that is liberal in ethos welcomes women as full partners in society, in marriage, and in ministry, and it sensitively seeks ways of demonstrating that in Christ there is neither male nor female.[12]

A truly liberal church is also a humble church. It is conscious of its own shortcomings and, instead of magnifying its successes, celebrates its constant need for mercy. When a Roman Catholic Church near my parish entered a period of renewal, they wrote to us as a congregation, asking us to pray for them. Would that more neighboring churches had the humility to do the same! Roman Catholics still do not officially recognize the validity of Anglican orders, but our neighbor parish recognized the validity of our prayers.[13]

SEMPER REFORMANDA

Fourthly, a liberal church is a reforming church. It is alert to the dangers of archaism. Archaism, a retreat into the past as a way of avoiding a troubling present, takes many forms. It may seek the pomp and ceremony of a bygone era, or resist in principle any change in the liturgy, or insist on only the older and more familiar hymns. Anglicans seem especially prone to this disease, despite the fact that the Articles of Religion, written in the sixteenth century, specifically say,

> It is not necessary that Traditions and Ceremonies be in all places one, and utterly like; for at all times they have been divers, and may be changed according to the diversities of countries, times, and men's manners, so that nothing be ordained against God's Word.[14]

A liberal church — as opposed to an archaic church — will be open to liturgical, musical and structural reform, as long as those reforms conform to God's Word.

Fifthly, a liberal church is a prophetic church. Seeking to understand the world and call it to account in the light of kingdom values, it takes seriously Jesus' call to be salt and light in the world and it is willing to take action to root out those ills which are the cause of misery for so many. With Avery Dulles I agree that the Church is an "agent of peace and justice in the world, [and] therefore it (is) appropriate for the ecclesiastical leadership to point out the dangers of dehumanization and to inspire concrete initiatives for the transformation of human society according to the ideals of the Kingdom of God." But Dulles is also right when he warns that the prophetic church is always in danger of "seeing man's final salvation within history" and therefore failing to see the "provisional character of any good or evil experienced within history."[15] There is the additional danger of pointing out only those ills which it is popular to criticize, and avoiding what is unpopular to condemn in society at large or unpleasant to deal with in the church. If a church has fallen victim to this tendency, you will easily be able to predict which evils it will denounce by reading the editorials of major daily papers.

Sixthly, a liberal church is a compassionate church. Someone has said that bread for myself is a material problem; but bread for other people is a spiritual problem. A liberal church takes servanthood seriously because it remembers that Jesus came to proclaim release to the captives, recovery of sight to the blind, to set at liberty those who are oppressed, and to proclaim the jubilee year of the Lord.[16] Therefore, whether it is medical supplies for the sick in the Third World, housing for the homeless in the first world, or just, loving relationships where people help each other by sharing gifts and offering practical help, the church is to be a place of compassion. While the church must always beware of apostasy dressed in the garb of sincerity or heresy sweetened with the saccharine of compassion, if it is not supremely a loving church it simply does not have the mark of Christ.

UNITY AND LIGHT

Seventhly, a liberal church is an ecumenical church. It remains justifiably skeptical of some aspects of the ecumenical movement, particularly the movement's tendency to bypass important matters of doctrine in its enthusiasm for organic union, its tendency towards syncretistic theologies (theologies that teach that "all religions are really the same, when it comes right down to it"), and its love affair with Third World movements advocating violence in the name of liberation.[17] But it is saddened by the scandal of our disunity. In the light of our Lord's prayer in John 17, why must there be 125 separate missionary societies serving in Japan alone? Ugandan bishop Festo Kivengere said: "By our denominationalism we tell the world how much we hate each other." The church must always echo Jesus' prayer that we may be one "in order that the world might believe."[18]

Finally, a liberal church is a positive church. Occasionally, it must be the foghorn that warns of dangers, especially when conditions are so bad that its light cannot be seen. But its first task is to be the light which points the way. Charles Colson, winner of the 1993 Templeton Award in Religion, tells of a riot in a prison in Washington, D.C. Inmates were torching buildings, and roaming around with guns, threatening guards. But in the middle of the prison yard, linking arms and singing hymns, a group of Christian inmates surrounded a group of guards and prisoners who had sought protection. Because of the brave witness of those men who chose to be lights in the midst of darkness, lives were saved. Here is a paradigm for the church today.

MR. GREATHEART

I identify Phillips Brooks with many of the positive features of liberal-mindedness. Although for a few years before his death he was the Bishop of Massachusetts, it was during his rectorship of Trinity Church, Boston, that he made his real mark. A legend in his time, he was held in such respect that once when he got on a streetcar, all conversation stopped while passengers stared in awe of the man whose preaching had captivated and touched the lives of so many.

Brooks was raised in a pious New England home and taught to love the Scriptures and memorize hymns as a young lad. His seminary training at Virginia Theological Seminary sought to reinforce the evangelical heritage which he brought with him, and in many ways he never left those evangelical roots. On one occasion in Boston, he substituted for the evangelist D.L.Moody who was sick during a crusade. Brooks sang the revivalistic hymns and preached powerfully on the conversion of St. Paul. He also took preaching missions in the poor north end of Boston where, after a huge choir sang a gospel song like "Just as I am", he would hold forth on repentance and faith.

Given the climate in which he worked and lived, and his immense popularity, it would have been surprising for Brooks to have been untouched by the liberal trends in theology which were increasingly fashionable in his day. He was influenced by Continental Romanticism, and placed much emphasis on the individual's conscience as a final court of appeal over against external authority. Conscience was crucial to Brooks' theology because it was his way of opposing the typical nineteenth century indifference to the social implications of the gospel. He was aware of the dangers inherent in his exposure to the liberal theological tendencies of his day. Yet he wanted very much to probe the foundations of the faith which he had inherited.

It was Brooks's deep understanding of the human condition which rightly earned him such a wide hearing, and made hundreds of his published sermons best sellers. As a preacher, he wrestled with human problems with which people could identify, and called people to the highest of which they were capable. In every man, he said, there is a dream of what he could be, which begins to come forth when he gives himself to Jesus Christ in consecration. "Break through the cross of your despair and ask Christ to let you see yourself as He sees you, all stained with sin but with the Divine image in you all the time."[19]

TOLERANCE

Brooks preached tolerance. However, he believed that tolerance was only possible when people had reached a spiritual level where they could see that truth was always larger than their own conception of it. Believing in the importance of the mind, he understood Jesus as wanting to persuade people of the truth rather than impose it from above.[20] His commitment to tolerance did not arise out of any indifference to truth. On the contrary, he maintained that to be tolerant one had to have something to be tolerant about.[21] He supported equal rights for women, and paid the price of some dear friendships because of it. He reached out in many ways to the poor and the working people, enlisting the help of hundreds in fighting the ills of society.

In churchmanship, Brooks believed that a Christian may be so bound by rites and ceremonies as to lose the God whom they are supposed to bring near. Liturgy should never substitute for the power of prayer, and no denomination should be so stuck on its historic ministry that it loses connection to the present ministry of Christ himself.

Phillips Brooks was a man as big in spirit as he was in body. He sought to combine New Testament Christianity with a liberality of thought which in his day opened many closed minds to the person of Christ and his call upon their life.

ENDNOTES

1 Lytton Strachey, *Eminent Victorians* (London: Penguin Books, 1948), p. 18-19.

2 Samuel Butler, *The Way of All Flesh* (London: Penguin Books, 1966), p. 94.

3 Dean M. Kelley, *Why Conservative Churches Are Growing: A Study in Sociology of Religion* (New York: Harper & Row, 1977) p. 147-8.

4 J.I. Packer, *Fundamentalism and The Word Of God* (Grand Rapids: Wm. B. Eerdmans, 1983) p. 153.

5 Eta Linnemann, *Historical Criticism of the Bible: Methodology or Ideology?* tr. Robert W. Yarborough, (Grand Rapids: Baker, 1990), p. 100.

6 Thomas C. Oden, *After Modernity...What?* (Grand Rapids: Zondervan, 1992) p. 41.

7 Rosemary Radford Ruether, *Sexism and God-Talk* (Boston: Beacon Press, 1983), p. 136. For a critique of feminist theology see "Christianity or Feminism?", Leslie Zeigler, *Speaking The Christian God*, ed. Alvin F. Kimmel, Jr. (Grand Rapids: Eerdmans, 1992), pp. 313-334. Also Donald G. Bloesch, *The Battle for the Trinity* (Ann Arbor: Servant, 1985), pp. 1-12.

8 Jn. 8:1-11. This passage is missing from many of the early Greek manuscripts of the Gospel, and would appear to have affinities with the synoptic Gospels. Located in different places in Luke and John in varying manuscripts, it doubtless preserves an authentic fragment of gospel material. See F.F. Bruce, *The Gospel of John* (Grand Rapids: Wm. B. Eerdmans, 1983), p. 413.

9 F.F.Bruce, *op. cit.*, p. 414.

10 Dietrich Bonhoeffer, *Life Together* (New York: Harper & Row, 1954), p. 110.

11 Mt. 13:28-30.

12 For those who read St. Paul differently, I draw attention to Richard N. Longenecker's *New Testament Social Ethics for Today* (Grand Rapids, Eerdmans, 1984), pp. 70-97. " ... we should not blame Paul too severely for failing to resolve all the tensions (between the categories of creation, stressing hierarchy and order, and of redemption) or solve all the difficulties, particularly since we seem to have done very little better in resolving them ourselves. On the contrary, we should applaud him for what he did do: he began to relate the theological categories of creation and redemption, most often emphasizing the latter, and he began to apply the gospel principles of freedom, mutuality, and equality to the situations of his day."

13 Pope Leo XIII rejected Anglican orders as invalid in "Apostolicae Curae" (1896).

14 Article XXXIV.

15 Avery Dulles, *Models of the Church* (New York: Doubleday, 1978) p. 179,202.

16 Lk.4:18.

17 "The contemporary campaign of abuse directed against the World Council of Churches is certainly predictable and perhaps even to be welcomed as a sign that the sharp sword of the word of God is piercing our complacence and challenging the comfortable syncretism in which our Western Christianity has been living for so long." Lesslie Newbigin, *Foolishness to the Greeks: The Gospel and Western Culture* (Grand Rapids: Eerdmans, 1986), p. 147-8.

18 Jn. 17:21.

19 Raymond W. Albright, *Focus on Infinity*, (New York: Macmillan, 1961), p. 308.

20 Ibid., p. 206.

21 Ibid., p. 277.

The World Is My Parish

For more than a decade Cyril Okorocha crisscrossed the Anglican Communion speaking, writing, motivating and networking among mission-minded Anglicans as a special emissary of the Archbishop of Canterbury. His many books still sharpen minds about the cutting edge of mission, and talking to him one gets the impression that here is a man with a deep passion for the Gospel. With his Ph.D. from the University of Aberdeen, and a wife who has her own earned doctorate in education and counseling, this fiftyish couple, with their four children, reflect the new face of Anglicanism: educated, traveled, urbane, gifted, and black. Convinced that this is God's time for Africa, Cyril Okorocha in 1999 moved back from the world stage to his home turf among the Igbo peoples of Southeastern Nigeria as the newly-elected Bishop of Owerri. His vision for Anglicanism, as for the whole church, is of a christo-centric, Scripto-centric, "rainbow fellowship," inclusive of people with diverse experiences of the Holy Spirit, but bearing a solid confession that Jesus Christ alone is Lord. Will Westerners hear the cry out of Africa for a church that is committed to evangelism, mission, and social transformation?

GLOBAL
The word of vision
and vitality
— ✤ ─────────────────

It was a foggy day with a thick mist covering the
channel between Catalina Island and the California
coastline. But veteran long-distance swimmer
Florence Chadwick, who had already swum the
English Channel both ways, slipped into the cold
Pacific waters determined to beat the men's record
for the 21 mile swim. It was July 4, 1952, and
millions watched the courageous champion on
national TV.

Florence was challenged by the numbing cold,
and the fog was so thick that she could barely see
her mother and trainer who were riding in a boat
nearby. Sharks came so close that they had to be
driven away with rifles; but Florence swam on.
Rarely was she dissuaded by fatigue; but the fog
and the cold did bother her.

At 15 hours, she was so numbed by the cold
that she asked to be taken out. But she was urged
not to quit, and told that she was near land.
However, when she looked up, all she could see
was fog. Fifteen minutes later, she was taken out
of the water. When she thawed out, she was told
the discouraging truth that she gave up just a half-
mile from land! It wasn't the fatigue, she told
reporters, nor the numbing cold. It was the fog. It

obscured her goal, effectively blinding her reason, her eyes, and her heart.[1]

A similar fog prevents many serious Christians from grasping a true picture of the church today. It is possible to read what has been written in this volume and still assume that the church we are called to believe in is the local church that most of us come in contact with week by week. Either we think of the building around the corner as "the church," or we think of the congregation of believing people that we belong to as "the church." But our vision of the church is much too narrow if it is bounded by the community of which we are a part.

This narrow fog-bound focus is soon to vanish. Part of the reason for this is sheer demographics. The average American moves fifteen times in the course of a lifetime. Although the rest of the developed world is somewhat less mobile, it is not far behind. With the erosion of denominational loyalty, the fragmentation of many nuclear families, and the changing economic situations of those born after World War II[2] -- for whom job prospects have taken precedence over regional loyalty -- the little church around the corner, even the big church downtown, or at the suburban crossroads, are scarcely able to retain the loyalty of coming generations. We have simply got to think bigger than our local scene.

But even a vision for the church on a national scale is too limited. The Christian church is now truly global. However, the awareness of American Christians can be bounded by the dimensions of the

United States. We need some experience or awareness of the church in the "two-thirds world" in order to understand what the church today is all about.

AN EYE-OPENING ENCOUNTER

My own vision of the global nature of the church occurred on a mission trip to the People's Republic of Angola. This African nation had once been the wealthiest on the continent; but now, after decades of civil war, it was one of the poorest. Garbage and filth lined the roads, even of the capitol city of Luanda with its once-glorious palm-lined riviera. When my daughter and I arrived, we immediately felt the oppressive hand of a Communist-run government with its mercenaries from Cuba in military fatigues, Russian MIGs flying overhead, and passengers boarding flights for distant places like Ponyang and Saigon.

But our hearts were cheered to meet missionaries caring in their simple hostel for travel-weary relief workers, and for the occasional Western visitors like ourselves. On Sunday morning they took us to church, which happened to take place in a roofless hut on the mud-covered city dump. But the people who had gathered from their tin covered shacks, and walked through rat-infested sewage to come seemed joyful – even radiant. Songs and readings sandwiched a hard-hitting sermon by an earnest African evangelist who spoke in Umbundu and whose words were translated into Portuguese. One bi-lingual missionary translated the Portuguese into French, and I, with my fractured French, did my

best to convey the essence to my then 18-year old
daughter.

What struck me was the hope in the eyes of these
believing people. Not bitter that the UN had
delayed by years building low-cost housing, not
mournful about the civil war which left thousands
dead and more thousands maimed by land mines,
and not envious of the relatively well-dressed
foreigners from America, they sang with hearts full
of joy, and filled the air with their praises to
Christ their Lord.

Here was the global church: thriving in the midst
of incredibly discouraging surroundings, winning the
battle for the souls of their despairing friends and
neighbors, and keeping the Faith in one of the
world's most miserable cess pools.

THE TWILIGHT OF TRUTH

A reasonable question to ask is, why so many
educated American Christians are unaware of the
global church? No doubt there are many reasons,
including lack of exposure, but an important
contributing factor to our ignorance can be summed
up in one word: post-modernism.

From the end of the 18th century to the 1960s
Westerner Europeans and North Americans have
lived in what has been called the modern era. One
aspect of the modern era is that, starting in the
French Enlightenment prior to the French
Revolution of 1792, Western intellectuals have
challenged the idea that there is such a thing as

revealed truth and have criticized religion as "backward."

Now, it should be noted that the Western intellectuals' views on religion have had little impact on the fate of religion in the world at large. Christianity grew phenomenally during this same period, both because of the modern missionary movement and because of the increasing adaptability of religious institutions following World War II. However, modernity as a world view has gradually pushed aside the traditional assumptions of Christendom in the Western world.[3]

Despite having different opinions from traditional Christians on very many subjects, the "modern" intellectuals did take over from their Christian forebears one central idea: they believed in a coherent view of truth. By that I mean that they believed that there were "answers" to questions and that these answers could be arrived at through the use of logic or inductive or deductive reasoning. Of course, they did not believe that answers could be arrived at through revelation, as in the Bible. But they believed that the answers they arrived at through reasoning processes were answers nonetheless. They thought that these answers were universal, the way that answers in mathematics are universal. In other words, all thoughtful people could arrive at the same answers if they used a process of reasoning and experimentation.

However, this fundamental assumption of modernity began to break apart in the late 20th century, as a result of the existentialist attack on reason, championed by such thinkers Sartre and Camus.

But the trend was most evident in Friedrich Nietzsche, the 19th century atheist German philosopher who announced the "death of God." Modernity's confidence in the universality of reason no longer seemed adequate to these European thinkers and writers. Those who saw themselves as post-modernists renounced the idea of universal answers that could be arrived at by means of reason, especially in the realm of meaning and values. The best one could say was that each person has their own unique experience, which is the lens through which they see reality. But that personal lens cannot be normative for anybody else.

A corollary of this view was soon to emerge, primarily via cultural anthropologists who studied cultures around the world. They claimed that there is no such thing as a universal human community that possesses something we could call "human nature." Nor is there any history or any tradition that unites all peoples across the centuries. To the contrary, the world is a patchwork of communities each of which develops a common set of assumptions and carries forward its own story.

The result of all this ferment was that truth, once considered a prized possession of all enlightened people, became essentially a dirty word. Increasingly one hears from philosophers that all claims to absolute truth are merely claims to power.[4] Truth, they say, is only used by those with economic, political and intellectual power as a means of reinforcing their own superiority.

It would be wrong, of course, not to admit that there is some justice in this. Western civilization has long assumed its own cultural preeminence, and has tied its own economic, industrial and now informational hegemony to those shaping ideas that gave birth to democracy and capitalism. In doing so it has overlooked the cultural contributions of non-western people, and ignored the intellectual heritage of non-Europeans.[5]

Although Christian intellectuals in the West may oppose post-modernism in principle, American churches are sometimes guilty of acting as if it were true. We do this when we assume that we can isolate ourselves from the church around the world, with our own story and our own way of telling it as the only one that matters for us.

THE STUBBORNNESS OF THE GOSPEL

We Christians must respond to the claim that there is no common human story, no common human nature, and no universal answer to the pervasive human hunger for truth. Post-modernism's claim that communities can do no more than give voice to their own stories is a direct contradiction of the message of the gospel. If there is one distinguishing trait of global Christianity it is a stubborn insistence that God's story of saving history transcends the limitations of any one culture.

Easterners and westerners, northerners and southerners, rich and poor, educated and illiterate, black, yellow, red and white - all have found a common link with Jesus Christ as revealed in the pages of the Bible. Quite naturally, they have expressed this unity through a diversity in worship patterns, ecclesiastical organizations, musical tastes, and distinctive readings of nonessential Scriptural verses that can be bewildering to the outsider. But the common confession that Jesus Christ is God and Savior[6] transcends particular cultures and ages. No other story has captured the imagination and loyalty of such a diverse worldwide community. This universality explains why the church of Jesus Christ is such a threat to totalitarian regimes everywhere and attracts persecution.

But in recent years the cultural and theological isolation of Western "First World" Protestants is breaking down, as the world becomes a global village. Linked through instant satellite communications, interlocking economies, travel and a shared ecosystem, Christians from every corner of the globe are meeting to discover how much they have in common, and how their destinies are bound together in ways previous generations would never have imagined.

SURPRISE IN CANTERBURY

The 1998 Lambeth Conference is an illustration of this new cooperation, and a signal of the new globalism that is emerging on the Christian landscape. Seven hundred and fifty bishops, spouses, and supporting personnel descended on the historic city of Canterbury southeast of London for three weeks of prayer, deliberation, and consultation that lasted from mid July to early August. The colorful display of episcopal purple in regal procession down the aisle of Canterbury's 12th Century cathedral, accompanied by the sound of ancient Gregorian chants, masked a very significant shift that was taking place within the Anglican Communion. A similar change is taking place in other worldwide bodies.

In Canterbury leadership was being passed from the Northern to the Southern Hemisphere.[7] Even the existence of this new leadership is not what many pundits had predicted. Younger churches planted by missionaries in Africa, Asia and Latin America, were as recently as the 1950's widely considered to be obsolete and dying because of their colonial associations. Yet it is precisely among these churches that we have seen explosive growth. Today there are more Anglican Christians worshipping each Sunday in Nigeria alone than in all of Europe, Britain, Canada and the United States. The same could be said of Uganda or several other parts of Africa. Nor can these African Christians be characterized as primitive, simple folk, only one generation removed from animism, as some of their racist Western detractors have maintained.[8] In fact, Nigeria's bishops are three times more likely to have earned doctorates than their American counterparts.

At Lambeth the new globalism was expressed in a number of resolutions that were passed with overwhelming support. By a margin of 7 to 1, the bishops said that sex belonged in lifelong heterosexual, monogamous marriage, thus dashing the hopes of Western liberals who had hoped that homosexual partnerships might be legitimized by the worldwide church. The impetus behind this

156

overwhelmingly conservative vote was not, as has been maintained, a collusion between "unenlightened" Africans and "mean spirited" American conservatives. Rather it was a recognition that the church is now global. One part of the church cannot operate in isolation from the rest.

Similarly, the outcry of those bishops from debt-ridden nations in the Southern Hemisphere for help in reducing the debt burden imposed upon their people by self-serving governments was clearly heard. These nations that borrowed heavily from Western sources now must repay huge loans at crushing interest rates. In many cases, corrupt leaders pocketed the money and the people are left with economic disaster. The attention that the Western churches paid to this issue was another sign of the growing influence of the churches of the south.

CONSCIENCE AND MISSION

The Conference also sent a strong message to the Western bishops that their own captivity to politically correct views on the ordination of women was a breach of conscience. Anglicans who still cannot accept the ordination of women have a right to be considered members in good standing within the Communion. Only a year earlier the American Episcopal Church passed Canon III.8.1, forcing dioceses which did not recognize the ordination of women to the priesthood and episcopate to change against their will or face reprisals. Flexing their new muscle, conservative bishops from other parts of the Anglican Communion sent a strong message to their Western brothers and sisters: move cautiously, and don't break the unity of the Communion over secondary matters. Alas, this message seems not to have been heard.

Other issues underscored the importance to the worldwide church of these younger, more mission-minded churches. For instance, while dialogue with other religions was welcomed, nothing was to stand in the way of the continued proclamation to the world that Jesus Christ is the Lord and Savior of all.[9] Also, special note was taken of the growing numbers of Christians who are suffering for their faith under hostile governments or in countries where governments are powerless or unwilling to confront extremist elements. Some of the bishops present bore the marks of harassment and even persecution for their faith, and many exist in places where their personal safety cannot be guaranteed.

MAKING HEADWAY PAINFULLY

The changes inherent in the culture and the challenges facing the church lead me to reflect on Mark 6:45-52. Here is a prism through which to ponder the nature of the Church in the coming century. Many have spoken and written of the parallels between our own times and those in which the early church first carried the gospel to the so-called pagan world.[10] These parallels encourage us to see in the New Testament a foreshadowing of the church in our times.

Immediately he made his disciples get into the boat and go before him to the other side, to Bethsaida , while he dismissed the crowd. And after he had taken leave of them, he went up on the mountain to pray. And when evening came, the boat was out on the sea, and he was alone on the land. And he saw that they were making headway painfully, for the wind was against them. And about the fourth watch of the night he came to them, walking on the sea. He meant to pass by them, but when they saw him walking on the sea they thought it was a ghost, and cried out; for they all saw him, and were terrified. But immediately he spoke to them and said, 'Take heart, it is I; have no fear.' And he got into the boat with them and the wind ceased. And they were utterly astonished, for they did not understand about the loaves, but their hearts were hardened.

This story of Jesus walking on the sea was doubtless included in the Gospels of Matthew, Mark and John because it encouraged the young church to move forward into an increasingly hostile environment. It must be distinguished from another famous gospel story with which it has some similarities, namely the occasion when Jesus stilled the storm. Here in Mark 6, there is no storm. Rather there is a persistent, discouraging, opposing wind buffeting a boat full of disciples who are tempted to think that Jesus had abandoned them.

Various scholars have pointed out that the historicity of this and other stories in no way suffers if we assume that they were included in the gospels because they spoke powerfully to the needs of the first century church.[11] So we are led to ask, what kind of a church might find this story especially meaningful? Probably not a church that is facing outright persecution. A real storm would be a better metaphor for persecution. Here the disciples are just dealing with wind; but it is a wind that is difficult to row against. This is the image of a church that is moving into an increasingly hostile culture.

Mark's story also speaks to a situation in which the church is beginning to sense a distance from Jesus.[12] He is on the shore. Before that, he is off in the hills somewhere praying. We are given a picture of a church in which people no longer feel that first excitement of faith which once brought Christ so near.

Then there are the waves. Waves symbolize problems that threaten to engulf the young church. She tries to keep rowing forward; but the waves are making things very difficult. On top of this, there is the darkness. In the darkness, we sense a picture of an eclipse of revelation – a time when the Word of God is not as clear as it once was, and where the dark world of paganism has begun to engulf the faithful and confuse their leadership. When Jesus does appear, in all his divine power and mystery, the disciples act like they are more afraid of him than they are of their own circumstances. Is this a church that is so out of touch with Jesus that it fears him in his supernatural power and majesty more than it does its own institutional demise?

But the good news in this story is found in two crucial elements. First, the disciples are making headway. It is painful, to be sure. But they are rowing hard against the winds of pagan society and making progress. And second, despite their preoccupation with their own problems, Jesus is not far off. He comes to them in all his ghostly luminescence, and declares: "It is I; have no fear."

LIVING BEYOND FEAR

Churches which have gained a global perspective and maintain lively global connections have a number of similar and important characteristics which reflect those found in Mark's story of Jesus walking on the water. These I would argue are the very characteristics that Anglicanism is beginning to embrace through the leadership given by Third World bishops and a younger generation of theologians from all over the world who are committed to a biblical and orthodox understanding of mission.

First, the new global churches are realistic about the nonchristian cultures in which the church now finds itself. This realism breeds a tough-minded determination to be faithful at all costs. And the costs are considerable. Thousands of Christians are martyred every year for little more than their refusal to abandon faith in Jesus Christ. Bishops and pastors live in the realization that at any time they might meet sudden death. Churches are bulldozed to the ground. Permits for missionaries or for new church buildings are routinely denied. Believers forfeit opportunities for advanced learning as a matter of course. Nor can these Christians look to Western governments to come to their aid. In many cases, the economic gain to Western governments through doing business with resource-rich persecutor nations far outweighs their vaunted concern for human rights. Indeed, some of these persecutor nations continue to benefit from lavish grants from countries where Christians are in the majority, and where religious minorities who have emigrated are protected by law.[13]

Second, the global church of the coming millenium will resist the siren call of religious pluralists. Yes, there is clearly a need for dialogue with representatives of other religions, especially where unnecessary tension exists due to ignorance and unfair stereotyping. But the church must not be deterred from its mission by a demand for religious pluralism that hides intellectual imperialism. Inherent in the call for tolerance that one sometimes hears in the West is the sterile assumption that other religions will adopt Western pluralist notions of truth anyway, once they see the light. In other words, while Muslim missionaries canvass continents for converts and an almost limitless array of nonchristian sects proliferate, enlightened Christians are expected to give up any idea that we might have a message for the world.

Global Christians know better. When veteran Anglican missionary and New Testament scholar Bishop Stephen Neill was asked what he thought of the idea that Christ might be the answer for Westerners, but not for adherents of other world religions, he replied: "Tell that to the converts." From the dawn of missions, the best evangelists have been those who have come to faith from some other system of belief. Indeed, if virtually everyone, even the atheist, operates from some implicit system of belief, then every true convert can say with the blind man of John chapter 9: "Once I was blind; but now I see."

A CONSERVING CHURCH

Thirdly, the church that has been captured by a global vision will be orthodox in doctrine. This conservatism, of course, runs in the face of those who prefer to let sleeping dogmas lie. But it cannot be denied that the 1998 Lambeth Conference was the most conservative Lambeth Conference of the 20th century. Paradoxically, it was also the most multi-cultural. The paradox cannot be attributed merely to the fact that the younger churches, founded by missionaries, have not yet reached the level of theological sophistication found in the West. Rather, in a global church, Christians cannot and do not operate in isolation from one another.

The elitism inherent in liberal theology works only when parts of the Body of Christ can say to the rest, "We have no need of you." In the global village the old test: "But will it play in Peoria?" is now applied universally. In core beliefs, as opposed to secondary matters, there must be mutual accountability. Since diversity cannot be the glue that holds us together, there must be basic unifying concepts that mark a community off as authentically Christian.

In an essay that is otherwise very inclusive, Andrew Wingate, a British theologian who has taught in South India, writes: "We would sensitively but firmly assert that fullness of relationship with God is possible only in Jesus

Christ, who is the definitive revelation of God."[14] That statement might easily serve as the very minimum that must be clearly articulated in today's pluralistic culture if the global church is to recognize a theologian as authentically Christian.

In Canada, for example, Essentials '94 sought to define the essentials of the faith for today. Seven hundred Anglicans from every province in the nation converged on Montreal for a five-day conference that produced The Montreal Declaration, plus a major book[15] and a dozen or more follow-up conferences -- some of which were better attended than the original -- as well as a flurry of other publications. Since that event, the great majority of bishops elected in Canada have been in basic agreement with the Essentials movement. This seems to indicate that even in the West theological orthodoxy is recovering its confidence, especially when advocates take care to articulate their views in a balanced and gracious way.

Fourthly, the coming global church will be strongly mission-minded. This will be inspired not only by Western missionaries heading east and south with the gospel, but by missionaries from the developing world reaching unreached ethnic groups in their own hemispheres and even sending missionaries to evangelize the jaded materialistic West. North America has already become a continent that receives missionaries. Africans, Indians, Chinese, Koreans and Latins, fired with the joy of the Lord, have already started criss-crossing America to evangelize not only their own ethnic groups but also secularized nominal Christians who have yet to discover the reality of Christ. In Nigeria, a new

Anglican missionary society has set its sights on sending missionaries to the largely Muslim nation of Niger and elsewhere overseas.[16]

Finally, the coming global church will intentionally travel light in respect to physical encumbrances. It will become more and more difficult to justify that new $250,000 organ, or lavish a substantial legacy on new plush carpeting for the sanctuary when a congregation is linked with a poorer congregation in another part of the world. As teams of lay people become accustomed to spending part of their vacation building an orphanage in an impoverished nation, or helping to develop discipling programs for burgeoning congregations of native believers, or supporting rehabilitation clinics for drug addicts in the inner city, they will become less tolerant of conspicuous consumption back home.

A CALL TO HOLINESS

As we envision all these challenges, we must recognize very frankly how difficult it is for churches to change. The trajectory of numerical decline and aging[17] will not easily be reversed, despite all the talk that goes on in clergy conferences these days about moving from "maintenance to mission."[18] With 70% of all Episcopal churches having fewer than 100 active members, the solution to our problems will have to go deeper and be more fundamental than is indicated by optimistic program ideas that stress welcome and inclusiveness.[19]

The bishop who ordained me thirty-eight years ago built churches in locations that are out of the way and virtually un-findable today. He did so because he truly believed that all parishes needed to do was hang up a sign saying "The Episcopal Church Welcomes You" and droves of people would find their way through the doors. We now know how wrong he was. People need more than a warm smile and a strong handshake to become living members of a Christian congregation.

While western churches struggle to hold on to members, they are surrounded by a culture that is fascinated by spirituality. Much of this spirituality is occult, new age, monistic and predictably trendy. It will pass. But there are still thousands who are hungering for spiritual reality, who are open to spiritual disciplines like fasting, prayer and solitude, and who yearn to find places where their quest can be nurtured in a community that is seriously dedicated to holiness. Unfortunately, like the disciples in the boat battling the strong winds, too many of us have hearts that are hardened.

With the disciples, we need a fresh vision of Jesus, and we need to face the fact that, unless the Lord is invited into the boat, he might just pass us by as he intended to do to them. Such an invitation must come from people who know that the darkness is not only in the culture around them, but it has penetrated their hearts and minds as well. We must invite Jesus in. This must come from converted people who have a hunger for holiness – that is, the intentional outworking of God's grace in the everyday events of our lives so that our characters reflect the likeness of Christ. Holiness is more than asking, "What would Jesus do?" in this or that crisis. It is the patterning of our lives around his priorities, and the conforming of our minds to the will of God, so that the ordinary events of our lives are caught up into his purposes.

Money, sex and power, the three classic areas of temptation, must become arenas where substantial victory is manifest. This is not a counsel of perfection. Instead, it is a call to God's people to become wise stewards of our wealth, to bring our unruly sex drives under the Spirit's control either through holy abstinence or in committed marriage, and to learn the discipline of submission and obedience, even while exercising leadership and employing spiritual gifts. These are not virtues to be gained by whips, chains and hair shirts; but by the realization that "God's love has been shed abroad in our hearts through the Holy Spirit who has been given to us." (Rom. 5:5) Once gained, they are rarely sustained in our lives apart from some sort of accountability group, wise spiritual direction, regular worship, and private daily time of quiet on our knees or in a chair with an open Bible.[20]

FAITHFUL ARE THE WOUNDS

Reactions to the 1998 Lambeth Conference by western bishops eager to see the worldwide Communion affirm an inclusive agenda which blesses same-sex unions and ordains homosexuals in committed relationships have sadly been predictably harsh. To them, the gospel is all about openness, standing alongside the marginalized, loving the outcast, supporting the rejected. And to be sure, there are many homosexuals among others who fall into these categories. Homosexuals are a stigmatized minority, and a concern for their fundamental human rights is an entirely Christian attitude.

However, the resolution restricting sex to heterosexual monogamy was passed at Lambeth by an overwhelming margin. This means that cries that the vote was manipulated by naïve Africans who were under the influence of "mean spirited" conservatives from the United States don't quite square with the facts. The decisive vote expressed a global concern for sexual holiness and reflects not just commitment to Christian orthodoxy, but distress over widespread permissiveness throughout the world, as manifested by AIDS in Africa, divorce in America, prostitution in Asia, and pornography in Europe. All these evils sap the moral fiber of nations and destructively undermine the foundations of civil society. The church cannot address this worldwide problem until its own house is in order. Thus the Lambeth resolution is a call to repentance in all areas of our sexual morality, and as such speaks prophetically to every one of us.[21]

A LEADER FOR TOMORROW

It is precisely this need for a prophetic voice in today's global church that leads me to think of Cyril Okorocha. The author of 7 books, and a graduate of University of London with an earned doctorate from Aberdeen University in Scotland, Cyril Okorocha believes that evangelism is the central task of the Church.

In his native Nigeria, where he has recently been elected Bishop of Owerri, the Church responded to the Decade of Evangelism in 1990 by consecrating and sending nine missionary bishops, in one day, into largely Islamic northern Nigeria to make disciples and share the love of Christ. Seeing themselves primarily as bearers of the Gospel vision and apostles of the Good News, they moved into the three existing northern Nigerian dioceses on the prayers of Christians from the south. These dioceses had very few Anglicans, so it was all pioneer missionary work. Astonishing conversions and church growth began to happen. Today there are eighteen dioceses where there were once only three, and more growth is anticipated.[22]

For years Cyril traveled throughout the Anglican Communion as the Archbishop of Canterbury's officer for mission and evangelism calling on parishes and dioceses to move from chaplaincy to prophetic voice. With his aristocratic Ibo bearing, urbane Oxford-sounding accent, and strong West African features, he caught the attention of bishops, priests and lay people around the world with workable strategies for raising up laity who were evangelists in their own communities. He especially highlighted the work of women and youth who often had the skills to carry the gospel forward, and stressed the importance of "doing" as well as "talking" the Good News.

The future of the worldwide church may rest with emerging leaders like Bishop Okorocha. Jovial, articulate, deeply in love with Jesus, and yet with the carriage and convictions of a true leader, he will help this historic church recover its zeal for evangelism and bring the deep spirituality of the African continent to many in the west who, unknowingly, are hungering for it.

It is also people like Bishop Okorocha who will help those of us mired in Western misunderstandings of the church to gain a new appreciation of its breadth and depth, and to rejoice in its vitality. As Dr. Christopher Seitz of St. Andrew's University in Scotland has said: "At the Lambeth Conference the words of a great hymn were realized, although it was not sung: 'In Christ there is no East or West in Him no South or North, but one great fellowship of love, throughout the whole wide earth.'"[23]

Or, in the words of Bishop Okorocha: "We need to broaden our vision in order to get into what God is doing. Evidence from Church history down the years shows that the Church is never at a standstill. Viewed globally, decline in one area is often a prophetic signal of growth in another. In the words of our Lord, we need to 'look up' to see that the 'fields are ripe and ready for harvest."[24]

ENDNOTES

1 Taken from Sourcebook of Wit and Wisdom, ed. Joe Taylor Ford (Canton: Communication Resources, Inc.), p.86.

2 Usually referred to as "baby boomers", with "Gen Xers" referring to those born after 1965.

3 The 19th and 20th Centuries have seen the greatest numerical expansion of Christianity since its inception.

4 Michael Foucault argues that the very idea of truth grows out of the interests of the powerful. Truth provides rational justification for the imprisonment, elimination, or dismissal of those who happen to contradict its general outlook. Alister McGrath comments that

"philosophy...becomes an accomplice in this repression by providing the oppressors with rational arguments to justify their practices." Pluralism and the Decade of Evangelism, Alister E. McGrath, Anvil, Vol. 9, No. 2, 1992 p.104-105. See Michael Foucault, Power/Knowledge: Selected Interviews and Other Writings, 1972-1977 (New York: Pantheon books, 1980).

5 The Persian Avicenna and the Arab Averroes, both Islamic scholars, exercised considerable influence on 11th and 12th Century understandings of Aristotle, for example.

6 Jesus Christ: God and Savior remains the doctrinal confession of the otherwise pluralistic World Council of Churches

7 "The Average Anglican is between 20 and 30, is brown-skinned, poor, lives in the two-thirds world, and is evangelical." Andrew Carey, The Church of England Newspaper, August 14, 1998. In the past 35 years the number of Anglicans in Africa has grown from 6 million to 26 million.

8 John Spong, the Bishop of Newark, claimed that the African Christians "have moved out of animism into a very superstitious kind of Christianity," and much post-Lambeth rhetoric has insultingly accused Africans of having been "bought" by chicken dinners and gifts of money.

9 Lambeth resolutions affirmed the priority of mission and evangelism, including the right of Anglicans to proselytize Muslims and other non-Christians.

10 Pagan comes from the Latin "paganus" meaning "country-dweller," just as heathen meant those who dwelt on the heath. Early Christianity was an urban phenomenon. Missionary expansion moved it out to the country areas.

11 N. T. Wright asks why, if the early church had made up stories about Jesus to address pastoral and ecclesial problems they were facing, they didn't make up stories to deal with those problems which we know from the epistles were besetting the early church? For instance, why are there no stories in the Gospels dealing with idol meat, widows, women's headgear, work, slavery, the place of Jerusalem within the wider Christian movement, and above all why is there virtually nothing about the detailed doctrines of Christ and the Holy Spirit? The New Testament and the People of God, N. T. Wright (Minneapolis: Fortress, 1992), pp. 420-427.

12 We may assume that Matthew, and probably even John, got the story from Mark. Luke, used to sailing on the ocean, would have

seen a high wind on Lake Galilee as a "tempest in a teapot," and perhaps for that reason omitted it.

13 As this chapter is being written, a report has been received of 1,200 Christians in Egypt who were illegally detained, raped, tortured, and even crucified. In 1999 Egypt received $2.5 billion from American taxpayers. Charles W. Colson, Breakpoint Commentary, November 10, 1998.

14 "Salvation and Other Faiths – An Anglican Perspective," in Anglicanism, A Global Communion, ed. A. Wingate, K. Ward, C. Pemberton, W. Sitshebo (New York: Church Publishing Incorporated, 1998), p.10.

15 Anglican Essentials, George Egerton, ed. (Toronto: Anglican Book Centre, 1995)

16 cf. Cyril Okorocha, "Evangelism in the Anglican Communion: An Overview," Anglicanism, A Gobal Communion, op cit., p.329.
17 The average Episcopalian is 57 years old.

18 Researchers Norman Shawchuck and Gustave Rath have argued that by 2050 60% of all existing Christian congregations in America will have disappeared. Benchmarks of Quality in the Church (Nashville: Abingdon, 1994), p.12.

19 Quoted in Toward 2015, A Church Odyssey, Richard Key and Roger White (Boston: Cowley, 1997), p.89.

20 Two excellent quiet time guides are the Scripture Union notes, which I have used for years, and the Bible Reading Fellowship, an Anglican plan. Scripture Union, P. O. Box 6720, Wayne, PA, 19087; and 1885 Clements Road, Unit 226, Pickering, Ontario, L1W3V4. Bible Reading Fellowship, P.O. Box M., Winter Park, FL, 32790.

21 The Conference "while rejecting homosexual practice as incompatible with Scripture, calls on all our people to minister pastorally and sensitively to all irrespective of sexual orientation and to condemn the irrational fear of homosexuals, violence within marriage and any trivialisation and commercialization of sex." The Conference also called upon members of the Communion to listen to the experience of homosexuals.

22 See Cyril Okorocha's account of this in "Evangelism – the Central Task of the Church", Anglicanism, A Global Communion, op cit., p.324.

23 A loose translation of Dr. Seitz's words at the S.E.A.D. Conference, Charleston, SC, January, 1999, in a paper entitled: "Does The Anglican Communion Have A Doctrine Of Scripture Post-Lambeth?"

24 G-CODE 2000, The Cutting Edge of Mission, A Report Of The Mid-point Review Of The Decade Of Evangelism, Cyril C. Okorocha, ed. (London: Anglican Communion Publications, 1996) p.13.

A call to comprehensiveness

Hannah More (1745-1833) was a noted English playwright and poet, who, in a day when it was unpopular to be serious about religion, combined her formidable accomplishments in these areas with deep Christian faith and social activism. A remarkable woman who counted as personal friends Samuel Johnson, Joshua Reynolds, Horace Walpole, Edmund Burke, and the famous Shakespearean actor David Garrick, Hannah More brought together evangelical piety, academic rigor, social concern and philanthropic effort. A leader in the revolution in personal morals which helped transform England from the poverty and decadence of the late eighteenth century into a place where slavery was abolished and popular education was available, she is remembered for her strength, grace and faith. What questions does this Anglican woman of nearly two centuries ago raise for those of us today who seek for that true comprehensiveness which Christ would have for his church?

ANGLICAN
A call to repentance and comprehensiveness

— ❖ ————————————————————————————

HANNAH MORE lived in a day when many were leaving the Anglican church for Methodism and/or other groups viewed by conventional society as sects for misguided enthusiasts. Since nearly everyone was expected to be a member of the established church in the late eighteenth century, it came about that serious Christian commitment was often expressed by a departure from the Church of England. One finds a similar dynamic occuring in South America today with the great exodus from the Roman Catholic Church by people touched by the pentecostal revivals there.

While I will return to Hannah More's story at the end of this chapter, it is worth mentioning in passing that people like More kept alive within the somnolent established church an earnestness about the relevance of piety to the issues of the day, and a conviction that biblical faith speaks plainly and powerfully to common folk. As a result, they helped make the Church the powerful influence it became in the second half of the nineteenth century.

The Modern Canterbury Trail

It seems that something of a reverse pilgrimage is taking place today. Richard Kew and Roger J. White point out in *New Millenium, New Church* that many evangelicals are leaving the denominations of their childhood and youth in search of a church that takes worship seriously, while at the same time over 600 former Roman Catholic priests are now ministering within the Episcopal Church.[1]

In Chapter 1 I mentioned Robert Webber, a professor at Wheaton College, who has written a book entitled *Evangelicals on the Canterbury Trail*, in which he interviews a number of people who have turned to the Episcopal Church from conservative evangelical churches. Webber, who is also a convert, has several introductory chapters describing his own pilgrimage to Anglicanism, including the reasons why he and the people he interviewed made the switch.

The reasons given are fairly predictable: a hunger for a more God-centered worship, a yearning to be linked with the primitive church, an appreciation for mystery, a sense of being spiritually fed through the eucharist, a place where people are accepted for who they are, and so on. Many who have come late to these things in their Christian journey will appreciate the zeal with which these converts share their discoveries.

However, one of these modern Canterbury pilgrims whom Webber interviewed caught my attention by likening himself to a boa constrictor, which swallows its prey whole and then proceeds to digest it. He seized upon Anglicanism "from an impulse of the heart" and swallowed it whole, without chewing. He was still digesting what he had swallowed. I read his story with interest, possibly because my own experience was so different from his. And the Anglicanism that this zestful convert had swallowed was not the sort that appeals to me.

He seems to have been very attracted to the colorful rituals of the Anglo-Catholic wing of the Anglican church. The Anglo-Catholic wing developed and flourished in the latter half of the last century. It was a reaction to the dreariness that marked many Anglican churches, where everything that created interest or promoted devotion in the worshiper seemed to be forbidden on the grounds that it was "Catholic." Many Catholic practices were reintroduced into Anglo-Catholic churches. This convert was strongly attached to the smells and bells, genuflections, daily masses, devotion to Christ in the consecrated elements, in fact, the whole apparatus of English Anglo-Catholic spirituality.

I recognize, of course, that some people will always be attracted to this form of devotion.

Moreover, Anglo-Catholicism must be credited for preserving some important emphases for the church —such as the dignity and centrality of sacramental worship. But as I approach my conclusion, I want to underscore the fact that the particular Canterbury Trail I have chosen myself and have frequently recommended to others does not involve the kind of uncritical, emotional suspension of judgment that I sense in the "boa constrictor" convert.

His, I think, was a conversion to mystery, authority, and tradition, in reaction to an evangelical upbringing that was seriously wanting in these areas of church life. But a reactionary attitude can blind us to the good in what we are leaving behind or the possible evils in what we embrace. The baby can be thrown out with the bath water. Precisely because Anglicanism is a fairly intellectual tradition, with many facets, it is perilously easy to grasp only that part which appeals to us and consider it sufficient.

PROCLAIMING THE GOSPEL, NOT THE CULTURE

Anglicanism attracts many people whose aesthetic sensibilities can no longer abide poor taste. The beauty of a well-choreographed service in an Episcopal church whose parishioners care for it, even if located in a poor area surrounded by an urban slum or a rural trailer park, makes a vivid contrast to what one finds in a typical independent or

179

Baptist church, with its theatre-like stage adorned with plastic flowers, and its gesticulating song leader with a necktie that looks like it would better belong on a Las Vegas emcee.

There is much to love in the Anglican heritage of British culture: pageantry, ceremony, color, and tradition. English church music holds a special appeal for many; and there is something unforgettable about boy choirs singing Gregorian chants in gothic cathedrals. But it would be tragic to think of Anglicanism merely as a church for waspish Anglophiles. The sheer demographics of who belongs to the Anglican church worldwide makes this ludicrous. There are more Anglicans in the world today who are black than white, and more whose native language is Swahili, Urdu, Hindi, Chinese, Japanese, and Spanish than Anglicans whose first language is English. The Anglican Church must never be allowed to become a sanctuary for monarchists who enjoy washing their mutton down with a glass of port. Those whose love of Anglicanism has a strong aesthetic dimension to it would be shocked to find increasing numbers of Church of England clerics in suit and tie leading contemporary worship in revamped sanctuaries void of pews, organ and robed choirs — at the main service on Sunday morning!

For the Anglican church to become the church God yearns for it to be, it must disengage itself from its British past and discover how to be thoroughly involved in twentieth century urban, North American culture (or in whatever culture it finds itself) while remaining thoroughly committed to Jesus Christ. However deeply thankful we might be for our ethnic roots, we must beware of baptizing our particular understanding of good taste and with it our assumption that Christian culture comes with a British accent. Our task is how to find a way to apply our commitment to excellence (in music, worship, architecture, ecclesiastical dress, and so on) to the culture in which we find ourselves. The process of adaptation and modification will not come easily to Christians who hold tradition in high esteem.

On a recent mission trip to Angola, I rejoiced to see the growth of the Angolan church. But I was also saddened to sit in churches and listen to twentieth century Africans singing nineteenth-century North American and European evangelical hymns that had been translated word for word, and note for note into Portuguese or Umbundu. Why must those Africans identify with a spirituality shaped by the romantic hymnody of Frances Ridley Havergal? Where were the drums, I asked my host? Where were the dancers? Where were the colorful African expressions of joy in the Lord? I was politely told that the young people were trying to bring these things in, but their elders frowned upon them as pagan.

Can we say "Thus saith the Lord"?

The Anglican church's tendency to confuse Christianity with a particular cultural expression is due in part to its short memory. While it cherishes traditions which have shaped the church theologically, spiritually, sacramentally and institutionally, it forgets that to the sixteenth century Reformers who shaped Anglicanism, all traditions are subservient to Scripture and are to be judged by it.

Because many Anglicans forget the priority which Anglicanism has given to the Bible, a seminary dean like the late Urban T. Holmes, III, can claim in his evocative book, *What is Anglicanism?* that Anglicanism need not rely on the Bible. He goes on to explain this by saying that the consciousness of Anglicanism is predominantly feminine. Anglicans, he argues, approach truth in an intuitive, communal, impressionistic way rather than a rational, logical, precise one, which he identifies as typically masculine. Holmes perpetuates the mistaken impression that Hooker's view of authority can be visualized as a three-legged stool of Scripture, Tradition, and Reason[2]. Holmes concludes that in authentic Anglicanism any statement preceded by "thus saith the Lord" will be extremely rare. Quite consistently, therefore, he finds no room in typical Anglicanism for either those emphases which have a clear idea of what the Lord *is* saying (Puritanism, Pietism, Evangelicalism) or those emphases which have a clear idea of what the Lord *isn't* saying (Latitudinarianism and Modernism). His view of what it means to be an Anglican eschews the idea of a confessional church which has specific teachings, despite the fact that the Creeds, Articles, Catechism, Homilies, and the Prayer Book all make confessional statements. Yet he is able to claim that pantheism, the idea that all creation is in God, is a classically Christian belief[3].

Consistent with his demotion of the Word of God and his pantheist view of creation, Holmes says that sacraments are to the church what sexual intercourse is to marriage. They guarantee nothing, he says, but rather are the seedbeds from which life in intimacy with God can spring.[4] This seems to me to put the cart before the horse. I would argue that, using his comparison to marriage, the sacraments are analogous more to the wedding service than the nuptial bed. They are — as Augustine called them — "visible words". By them, God's promises of accepting love, which are grounded in Scripture, are guaranteed to us. The sacraments, together with the exegetical word preached from the Scriptures, are precisely the "thus saith the Lord" to which the church is called to respond in faithful obedience. Intimacy with God is discovered and lives transformed by this clear proclamation of grace. Without this clear word, the Anglican church will continue to produce the dilettante clergy and bigoted laity that Holmes sees as the Church's besetting disease.

If Anglicanism is not to be distinguished by a feminine approach to truth, what then are its unique features? How is Anglicanism different from, say, Presbyterianism, or Congregationalism, or Lutheranism, or Anabaptism, or the myriad of churches that make up the patchwork quilt that is known as Christianity around the world? Anglicanism is not distinguished by having a systematic theology like the Presbyterians with their Westminster Confession and Calvin's Institutes. We do have the Thirty-Nine Articles; but while they define the parameters of our faith in relation to historic Roman Catholicism and Puritanism, they aren't intended to be a comprehensive theology. Nor is Anglicanism distinguished by a heavy doctrinal tradition like the Lutherans, although of course, everything in Anglican worship is undergirded by doctrinal assumptions, which, when you examine them, are not all that far from those of the Lutherans. Nor does Anglicanism have special emphases like the Anabaptists with their believer's baptism, or the Quakers with their inner light, or the holiness churches with their second blessing, or the Congregationalists with their democratic form of government.

MAJORING IN THE MAJORS

The essential contribution of the Anglican way is found in its distinction between things essential and things indifferent. The Anglican watchwords are unity, diversity, and charity: "unity in essentials, diversity in nonessentials, and charity in all things." The Anglican church sees itself as a church that majors in the majors, and minors in the minors. You might call it a "fundamentals-ist" church, to be distinguished from a fundamentalist church. The Anglican church's historic critique of the Church of Rome is based on the conviction that Rome has departed from the basics — the standards of the early Fathers, the Apostles, and Christ. Bishop Jewel (1522-1571), who prepared Richard Hooker for university, wrote that "we have called home again to the original and first foundation" which the medieval church had corrupted. [5] By the same token, Anglicanism's historic critique of many of the post-Reformation churches is that they neglect the core of the Apostolic tradition by stressing their own particular emphases.

The Anglican way is what C.S. Lewis called Mere Christianity, or what John Stott called Basic Christianity. Anglicanism deliberately seeks to concentrate its worship on the person of Christ, its witness on the biblical testimony to Christ, and its discipleship on obedience to the word of Christ.

This is why it is against the spirit of Anglicanism to make the views Christians have on the nature of holiness, the place of prophecy, the presence of Christ in the sacrament, the right kind of ecclesial government, the honors due to the Virgin Mary, or the inerrancy of Scripture a test of orthodoxy. The Anglican way focuses on the fundamentals. We say that, while these other issues are important, they are not foundational to the Faith.

This avoidance of controversy over minor issues translates into a healthy pragmatism. On a key issue like "How can I find a gracious God?" Anglicans have answered with one voice together with the great continental Reformers, to whom this was the first great question. However, on the second question of the Reformation, "Where can I find the true Church?" the Anglican answer was more tentative. Anglicans rejected both the biblical idealism of the Puritans, and the conservative traditionalism of the Catholics. Instead, Anglicans said there are no structural safeguards that will ensure the purity of Truth for all time. The church exists under grace, and purity must be accepted by faith rather than legislated by ordinance.[6]

This all begins to sound rather good, at least in theory. For instance, in 1930 the Lambeth Conference of bishops described the main ingredients of

186

Anglicanism as first, an open, available, unchained Bible; second, a common worship led by the whole priestly body of the church; third, a pastoral rather than a sacerdotal ministry (that is, one which emphasizes the dispensing of sacraments) or a didactic ministry (that is, one which emphasizes preaching); and fourth a fearless love of truth and a standard of conduct consistent with it. The only problem with this summation, as one writer put it, is that "too many interpreters of Anglicanism have spoken as though the ideal and the actual were one!"[7]

The fact of the matter is that the Anglican church has fallen disastrously short of its own goals in precisely those areas where it could have been strong. For most Anglicans, the Bible is not so much an unchained book as it is an unread and unknown book. At typical Anglican churches, worship is perfunctory and is solidly in the hands of professionals. The ministry is increasingly clerical, concerned mainly with the correct performance of ritual, despite the fact that great numbers of laity remain effectively unevangelized. Instead of a fearless love of truth, there is a fearful compromise on the basics of the Gospel. And a uniquely Anglican standard of conduct often cannot be identified, because it is barely distinguishable from the behavior of the secular world. Writing for the many who have abandoned the Anglican church in disgust, Sam Shoemaker, the noted and controversial rector of Calvary Episcopal Church in Pittsburgh, once said:

> They have seen sham and snobbishness during the hour of worship, when surely the spirit of Christ should be on us all. They have found church officers and pillars without spiritual enthusiasm, unwilling to see Christ's principles applied in their own business. They have seen plaster preachers, with tame ways and queer clothes, and heard them preach tepid, impossible pap from Christ's pulpits, or stroke a fat congregation with the rewards of a virtuous life and the blessedness of immortality, while two blocks away lie great festering sores of huddled humanity without a decent chance to draw a breath of clean air. And they have said, "We can't swallow that, and we won't!"[8]

Shoemaker is best remembered for his longing to make Pittsburgh as famous for God as it was for steel.

THREE ERRORS

So then where does Anglicanism go wrong? Why does it so rarely live up to its vision? Let me suggest three reasons.

Sweet Reasonableness vs. Spiritual Wisdom

First, Anglicans have mistaken sweet reasonableness for spiritual wisdom. There has been a love affair with secular knowledge, going right back to a man named Erasmus. Erasmus, who held a chair at Cambridge for a time, was probably the most brilliant man in Europe. His views on many subjects, for example, his support for religious toleration and for classical and modern learning, were widely respected in England. But he rejected Luther's view of the bondage of the human will, and stressed instead free will and our ability to live a simple, undogmatic, practical Christian life. His unwillingness to accept the serious nature of sin in the sixteenth century influenced the English church more than it realizes.

Ever since Erasmus, the majority of Anglicans have had an uncritical view of secular knowledge and the culture that it has spawned. Too many have refused to see that secular knowledge and the gospel of Christ are often in fundamental disagreement, and certainly operate on assumptions formed from totally different world views. Evangelicals within the Anglican church have always had a suspicion of high culture;[9] but this has not been a majority opinion. The consequence is that the richness of classical Christian wisdom, rooted in the Bible and tradition, is bypassed for vapid current theories from the humanities and the social sciences. Since all heresy begins with an inadequate view of sin, Anglicanism tends to teeter on the brink of heresy because it is unwilling to accept the Bible's own analysis of the human problem. Of this Anglicanism must repent.

The reticence of many major thinkers in the Anglican church to criticize educated opinion reveals an underlying unwillingness to submit the mind to God's word. As Luther said to Erasmus, "The difference between you and me, Erasmus, is that you sit above Scripture and judge it, while I sit under Scripture and let it judge me!" In the recent debate on sexuality between Bishop John Spong of Newark and John Stott, Rector Emeritus of All Souls, Langham Place, it was clear that the Bishop wanted in no way to tie his understanding of sexuality to what he saw as an outmoded biblical world view, but to draw his sexual ethics from the life situations of contemporary people. Stott, however, argued for the Bible's continued relevance and authority.[10]

Anglicans need to rediscover that Christ is not only the source and summation of all the wisdom to be found in other world views, but also its judge. The task of the Christian is, as St. Paul said, to "take every thought captive to Jesus Christ." [11]

Party Spirit vs. Godly Zeal

Secondly, Anglicanism has confused party spirit with godly zeal. The Anglican hierarchy would not accept the eighteenth century evangelical revival under the Wesleys and Whitefield. Had it done so, perhaps there would have been a permanent place within

Anglicanism for the godly zeal which Ronald Knox dubbed "enthusiasm." Certainly, the root concern of enthusiasts, that the "absolute ... remain absolute, (and) the relative (be) merely relative" is healthy.[12] And while everyone agrees that there are extremes to be guarded against when religious emotion is permitted free play, the fact is that from the day of Pentecost onward the Spirit of God has often manifested himself as a kind of holy intoxication. Jonathan Edwards wrote: "Without earnestness there is no getting along in that narrow way that leads to life."[13] Anglicanism has a habit, however, of writing off godly zeal as mere fanaticism. It scorns intensity. Instead of welcoming zeal, it insists on so close an association between nature and grace that it is uncomfortable with crisis types of holiness, and looks instead only for gradual moral improvement. What this means in practice is that Anglicans reserve their passions for secondary things: the pros and cons of liturgical revision; the differences between high, broad, and low churchmanship; and the theological fads or political and social issues that are the current rage. Party spirit replaces godly zeal; and the unity and fullness of the church is torn into little sections, some of which barely speak to each other. From such misplaced emotion, Anglicanism must repent.

One reason the Anglican church has had such a limited appeal to adolescents is its failure to comprehend the alternating depths and heights which characterize the teen-ager's emotional make-up. Emotional growth in the adolescent takes place not in slow increments but in fits and starts, and through experiences of high drama and deep despair. The twice-born spirituality of the Augustines, Pascals, Wesleys and Whitefields, while having an inherent appeal to adolescents, as well as solid scriptural grounding, yields an excitement for spiritual growth which few Anglican clergy know how to handle. For example, I recall reading Malcolm Muggeridge's description of his attempted suicide at a time of despair while a member of the British Secret Service in Mozambique towards the end of World War II. He describes swimming out into the Indian Ocean under the black African night sky, with no intention of returning, only to be arrested by the cruciform or cross-like shape in the water of the lights from two coastal cafes. Then, stricken with an intense sense of good and evil, light and darkness, compelled to return to the distant shore, an experience he describes as "one of those deep changes which take place in our lives ... a kind of spiritual adolescence." I wonder if his post-conversion departure from Anglicanism to Rome had something to do with his frustration over a church that had so little understanding of the ecstasy that his discovery of Jesus sparked.[14]

Balance vs. Comprehensiveness

Thirdly, Anglicanism confuses balance with comprehensiveness. It is easy to make this mistake. After all, as the middle way between Roman Catholicism and Puritanism, the Anglican church has tried to hold in tension many aspects of Christianity that other groups have rent asunder. On theological issues, there are the classic tensions between word and sacrament, or between incarnation and atonement. On Christian living, there are the tensions between prayer and action, evangelism and social service. On church issues, traditionalism versus radicalism are reflected in tensions between organization and organism, form and freedom. Beneath all these tensions lie the psychological polarities of head and heart, left brain and right brain, and order and chaos. Anyone who tries to hold together these differing emphases can end up trying to juggle so many things that nothing of any importance gets the full attention it deserves.

But as Charles Simeon of Cambridge once said, referring to the controversy between predestination and free will, "truth often lies not in the mean point between two extremes, but at both extremes!" Shouldn't this be what is meant by comprehensiveness? Why must we choose between evangelism and social action? But Anglicanism, instead of holding together prophetic and priestly religion in a way that respects both charismatic and institutional impulses, spawns myriads of separate movements. These in turn create further movements, prompting someone to comment that if the Episcopal Church in America has any more movements it will have diarrhea! For its failure to be as truly comprehensive as it ought to be, Anglicanism needs to repent.[15]

TRUE COMPREHENSIVENESS

If we take Peter's vision of the church as a model of the kind of comprehensiveness to which all churches should aspire, we will discover virtually all of the elements of the church which have been discussed in this book in embryo.

> Come to him, to that living stone, rejected by men but in God's sight chosen and precious; and like living stones be yourselves built into a spiritual house, to be a holy priesthood, to offer spiritual sacrifices acceptable to God through Jesus Christ. For it stands in scripture, "Behold I am laying in Zion a stone, a cornerstone chosen and precious, and he who believes in him will not be put to shame." To you therefore who believe, he is precious, but for those who do not believe, "the very stone which the builders rejected has become the head of the corner," and "A stone that will make men stumble, a rock that will make them fall"; for they stumble because they disobey the word, as they were destined to do. But you are a chosen race, a royal priesthood, a holy nation, God's own people, that you may declare the wonderful deeds

194

of him who called you out of darkness into his marvelous light. Once you were no people but now you are God's people; once you had not received mercy but now you have received mercy.[16]

Note the following elements which quite naturally arise from this text:

• *The church is evangelical*. Each individual who comes to Christ begins the spiritual pilgrimage. Each is discovered to be precious, and is sent forth into the darkness to bear witness to the light.

• *The church is catholic*. It retains the shape of the old Israel. It maintains organic continuity with the past and recognizes the priestly function of corporate worship.

• *The church is reformed*. God is sovereign in his calling of us into a covenanted relationship with himself. We are a chosen race in which priesthood is shared by all believers. We are a church which takes its stand on Scripture.

• *The church is charismatic*. Jesus Christ as head is at the very center, and the temple he is building consists of living stones, that is, of people made alive by the indwelling Holy Spirit.

• *The church is liberal*. Mercy is at its heart. Outcasts are welcomed into its bosom. The old Israel with its civil laws and cultic practices is replaced by a new trans-national, trans-racial nation that witnesses to the God who overcomes traditional barriers.

This is the comprehensiveness that I would wish for those who set out on the modern Canterbury Trail. This is an Anglicanism that is worth striving for, and towards which each member, with his or her own experience of Christ, should be happy to make a contribution. Peter's church is mission-oriented, sacramentally united, biblically grounded, Spirit-filled, and servant-minded. I can believe in this church and I want to be a part of it. The dream I have is that a humbled and renewed Anglicanism might give herself to the future church as a living model of what true comprehensiveness should be. To do so, Anglicanism must repent of its compromise with secular knowledge, its fragmenting party spirit, and its immobilizing fear of imbalance. Above all, it must listen again to the Scriptures which call us to be the church.

A WOMAN OF PARTS

As an example of true comprehensiveness, I have chosen as my final hero Hannah More. Although a private girls' school in Maryland was appropriately named after her, her name is not well known to-day. She was an unmarried laywoman (although she had many suitors) who was famous in her day as an educator, a noted playwright, and author.
Hannah More was clearly one of the most remarkable women in early nineteenth century English

society. She began her career by writing full-length plays geared to the upper classes. Immediately, she made a huge splash in literary circles. But as her Christian faith matured, she was drawn into the Clapham Sect, a circle of Anglican evangelicals who combined a love of the gospel with a deep social concern. Led by William Wilberforce, the Clapham Sect launched attacks first on the institution of slavery, and then on a wide range of social ills, including the lack of free public education. Within this group, Hannah More's spiritual mentor was John Newton, the converted slave trader. It was with his and others' encouragement that she began writing works of practical Christian piety and morals. These had an immense impact, as did the hundreds of pamphlets that she wrote for less educated readers. In all, her collected works filled eleven volumes when they were published in 1853.

But Hannah More was not just a writer and a deeply pious woman, she was an activist as well. Profoundly moved by the fact that the poorer children in rural areas had no educational opportunities, with Wilberforce's financial help she began a school in her own county, where the social conditions were terrible. This led to other schools, which began to show amazing results, despite the active opposition of the landed gentry who believed that education encouraged laziness. Literacy improved markedly, so much so that even parents came to take courses in the evenings. Soon her schools became models for other parts of the country.

Although Hannah More's work took her into the homes of nobility, literati, and even royalty, she was not afraid to identify with the unpopular evangelical wing of the Church of England. She was a strong woman with a mind of her own. When criticized by some of her conservative friends for joining the Society for the Propagation of Christian Knowledge (SPCK) because they distributed copies of the Bible with the Apocrypha, she replied "Better a Bible with an Apocrypha than no Bible at all!" Hannah More supported missions, helped form the Religious Tract Society, and was deeply concerned with women's issues. Above all, she sought to relate faith to character, piety to practice, worship to action, and the gospel to culture. I therefore choose Hannah More as my quintessential Anglican. Combining head and heart, she probably had more of an impact in her day than any prelate. Her gifts enriched both church and society, and her moral vigilance raised the standards of social and religious life from the Queen to common labourers.[17]

Here, then, is a church to believe in: evangelical in experience, catholic in spirit, reformed in doctrine, charismatic in ministry, and liberal in ethos. I walk the Canterbury Trail by choice because I believe the way is broad where the church should be broad and narrow where it ought to be narrow. It is far from ideal. But in the grace and providence of God, it has the potential of becoming the truly comprehensive church that is envisioned in the New Testament.

ENDNOTES

1 Cambridge, Cowley, 1992, p. 89-98.

2 See my comments on Hooker's view of authority in Chapter 3 on the "catholic" church. Also, my booklet, "The Authority of Scripture," published by Episcopalians United.

3 Urban T. Holmes, III, *What is Anglicanism?* (Toronto: Anglican Book Centre, 1982), p. 27.

4 Ibid, p. 37.

5 Stephen Sykes and John Booty, eds., *The Study of Anglicanism* (Minneapolis: SPCK/Fortress,1988), p. 233.

6 Ibid., p. 224.

7 Ibid., p. 415.

8 Samuel M. Shoemaker, *A Young Man's View of the Ministry* (New York: Federal Council of Churches and Association Press, 1923) p.23.

9 "The Agony of the Episcopal Church," Part II, William Coats, *Plumbline*, April, 1980.

10 Debate held in Vancouver, 1993. A videotape of this debate is available through Regent College, University of British Columbia.

11 2 Cor. 10:5.

12 Karl Rahner, ed. *Encyclopedia of Theology* (New York: Seabury, 1975) p. 432.

13 Donald G. Bloesch, *Essentials of Evangelical Theology*, Vol 2 (New York: Harper & Row, 1979), p. 43.

14 Malcolm Muggeridge, *The Infernal Grove, Chronicles of Wasted Time:* Number 2 (New York: William Morrow & Co., 1974), p. 183-5.

15 Philip Thomas writes, "talk of Anglicanism's doctrinal comprehensiveness is (quite often) a mask to cover doctrinal indifference." *The Study of Anglicanism*, Ibid., p. 230.

16 I Pet. 2:4-10.

17 "Let Us Now Praise Famous Women", an unpublished article by Peggy Noll; *Christian Spirituality*, ed. Frank N. Magill & Ian P. McGreal (San Francisco: Harper, 1988); *A History of the Church in England*, J.R.H. Moorman (New York:Morehouse-Barlow, 1959); *A History of the Evangelical Party in the Church of England*, G.R.Balleine (London: Church Book Room Press, 1951).

CONCLUSION:
Seeing the connections
———✹—————————————————

Each of the six words which I have used to describe
the church are each held in special honor by
different branches of the church universal. Together
they describe what appears to me to be the ideal
church - a church which is truly comprehensive and
which consequently gives adequate expression to the
various strands of the church found in the New
Testament.

Non-Anglicans may object that I have merely
presented an apologia for my own denomination. But
I would be content if they would reflect simply on
each of the six words I have used and substitute
for my Anglican heroes people from their own
traditions. In self-defense, I must also point out that
the Anglicanism which I commend in these chapters
will appear to many of my fellow Episcopalians as
remarkably un-Anglican. That is because the Anglican
church that I see in the future will be less culturally
English, less self-confident, less partisan, less in love
with the spirit of the age and more committed to
holiness, biblical orthodoxy, and compassion for the
fallen and the outsider than most would find in the
typical Episcopal parish down the road today.

INTER-ACTION BETWEEN THE CONCEPTS

How do these seven highlighted words that should be descriptive of every church relate to each other?

Unfortunately, we cannot assume that the gospel is at the center. Many reduce the full New Testament witness to a canon within the canon, or a gospel within the Gospel. The saving acts of God in the incarnation, cross, resurrection-ascension, sealing of the Spirit and coming again of Christ are given no normative place in the life and teaching of many churches. They are simply liturgical themes or symbolic illustrations of the real "gospel" which is that God loves and accepts us as we are, and wants us to be caring towards one another and to work for change in the world. For this reason I have attempted to draw out some of the implications of the Gospel in the first chapter as they relate specifically to a certain kind of spirituality.

There is another reason for placing the Gospel at the center of our understanding of the church. When the Gospel is at the center, the other dimensions of the church, which exist in a natural tension with each other, remain together, instead of pulling apart. Thus the Gospel becomes the centripetal force which keeps aspects of the church from breaking away from each other, to their mutual harm.

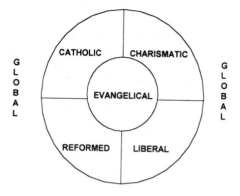

When the church has the Gospel or Evangel as its center of gravity the other dimensions are kept in harmony. Catholicity brings continuity, which is essential for nourishing our sense of our being a part of God's historic plan through the ages. The reformed emphasis clarifies doctrine, which is essential for disciplining the mind and schooling the emotions. The liberal dimension puts love for the poor and needy into what might otherwise be a self-centered church, and liberates the church to celebrate the wideness of God's mercy. Charismatic experience and ministry lead to openness to the presence of God, especially in worship, and to an immediate contact with the power of God which transforms and heals.

Furthermore, the Gospel at the center keeps the outer edges of the church from hardening. The catholic dimension is kept from becoming quaint, the reformed dimension from becoming doctrinaire, the charismatic dimension from becoming cultic, and the liberal dimension from becoming sentimental.

LEFT BRAIN AND RIGHT BRAIN THINKING

Holding these dimensions together is not easy. The catholic and reformed emphases relate primarily to our left-brain. That is, they tend to be objective, logical, reasonable, clear and linear. On the other hand, the liberal and charismatic emphases relate primarily to our right-brain. They are subjective, intuitive, active, murky and rhapsodic. Without each, the circumference (which is where outsiders first encounter the church, and where the church faces the world) becomes lopsided. The Gospel provides the needed balance. Liberal thinking tends towards inclusivity, and reformed thinking tends towards exclusivity. Both are needed, for the Gospel accepts us as we are, but calls us to be what God wants us to be. Similarly, the catholic direction is from outward to inward, while the charismatic direction is from inward to outward. But since the church is both organization and organism, it must be experienced as both to be fully grasped.

But just as each dimension seeks to pull away from its opposite, so it also yearns for it. Reformed and liberal yearn for each other, just as head and heart do. Yet they are naturally suspicious of each other. Similarly, catholic and charismatic yearn for each other, as the Catholic Charismatic movement testifies, and yet each views the other with suspicion also.

Finally, there is no completeness without all four dimensions. The reformed, liberal and charismatic need the catholic sacramental emphasis to grow up to maturity. The catholic, reformed and charismatic need the humanizing emphasis of the liberal in order to focus outward on the world for which Christ died. The catholic, liberal and charismatic need the reformed emphasis on the development of the intellect in order to fully worship God in truth as well as spirit. The reformed, catholic and liberal need the charismatic emphasis on life in the Spirit in order to be saved from the perils of relying on their own strength.

Moreover, when the church really sees itself as global, and accepts all those of whatever denominational stripe, who love the Father, the Son and the Spirit as brothers and sisters, it sees that its own health depends upon learning from believers who have managed to keep all these dimensions in proper tension. It refuses to rest content with those who have turned them into parties or even whole denominations, and longs and works for that wholeness which the Spirit intends.

THE CHALLENGE OF CHANGE – ARE WE PREPARED FOR IT?

The challenge to each congregation is to grow into the fullness that is our inheritance in Christ. But change is hard work. As others have said, the seven last words of the church, are "it's never been done that way before!" Anglicans seem particularly resistant to change; but I suspect that others may see their own traditions as equally stubborn.

Challenged to think of which Bible character might have made the best Anglican, Episcopal layman Byron Rushing, a member of the Massachusetts state legislature, once told a crowd that, in his opinion,

Jonah must have been the Anglican. First of all, when God told Jonah which way to go, he immediately went the opposite direction. Secondly, Jonah apparently had the wherewithal to pay his fare to the other end of the Mediterranean. Thirdly, when God finally got his attention, Jonah decided that maybe he would do it God's way after all. And finally, when God graciously gave Nineveh a stay of execution through the preaching of Jonah, Jonah went into a sulk. Like most Anglicans, Jonah knew that if he really did what God wanted, God would more than fulfill his side of the bargain and people would flood the church in search of new life.

But like most Anglicans, Jonah was simply not prepared for that. Fortunately, God was patient and persistent, and Jonah - we think - eventually saw it God's way.

STUDY GUIDE

The following study guide has been prepared for groups wishing to use this book as a resource for small group discussion. The questions below relate primarily to the major biblical passage that is quoted in each chapter. Group leaders may wish to add their own questions on the overall content of the chapter.

EVANGELICAL
The word of promise and challenge
(Hebrews 10:19-25)

1. Describe some of your feelings as you enter church and prepare yourself for worship.
2. Why was "entering the sanctuary" such an awesome prospect for Jews? (cf. Lev. 16:1-19)
3. In what sense is the cross central to the meaning of this passage? To the meaning of your life?
4. What role does baptism play in the ongoing life of faith? (cf. v.39)
5. What are the alternatives to "holding fast the confession of our faith"?
6. Think of three practical examples of how believers "stir one another to love and good works."

7. What themes in this passage speak primarily to the church, and what ones speak primarily to the individual?

8. What would you change in your church to make it recognizable as the body of Christ to the writer of this passage?

CATHOLIC
The word of continuity and balance
(James 5:13-20)

1. When you are desperately ill, who do you want by your bedside: the hospital chaplain in a clerical collar; your best friend; a member of your family; an intercessory prayer group from church; a faith healer? Someone else? Why?

2. Why is it important for the sick person to issue the invitation?

3. What is meant by "the prayer of faith"? — the prayer of those who believe that the person will get well? — the prayer of the sick person, offered in confidence of healing? — the prayer that arises out of faith in Christ? — the prayer offered by someone who has the gift of faith? (I Cor. 12:9) — Something else?

4. How would you help a suffering person to examine themselves for possible sin in their life?

5. What conditions for effective prayer are spelled out here?

6. Distinguish wandering from the truth from denying the truth. (Cf. Heb. 6:4-6; 10:26-31)

7. How do you help someone who is professing to follow Christ while living in disobedience to him — without appearing to meddle?

REFORMED
The word of freedom and truth
(Galatians 2:15-21)

1. How did the Jewish sense of chosenness make "justification" a troublesome problem? (v.15)

2. "Justified" means what?: — reckoned righteous? — made righteous? — a combination of the two? Can you support your view from other scriptures, not from Galatians?

3. Why is "faith" so easily turned into a good work, a work which the law requires?

4. Why can no one be justified by works of the law?

5. How does Paul risk being a "sinner" by insisting on justification by faith in Christ? (cf. 5:1-7)

6. How did Paul "die to the law", and why was that such a freeing experience for him? (cf. Rom. 7:4-6; 8:2)

7. Will the real Paul please stand up! Which is the real Paul in v. 20?

8. Are there ways in which the church nullifies the grace of God today?

CHARISMATIC
The word of life and power
(Acts 11:19-30)

1. Have you ever been to a charismatic or Pentecostal service? What were your impressions — both
positive and negative?
2. Find Cyprus, Cyrene, and Antioch on a Bible
map. Why were these important places?
3. "The hand of the Lord was with them" — what
is implied by the use of the word "hand" here?
4. What did Barnabas "see" in Antioch?
5. What were Barnabas' gifts and how were they
different from Paul's? Why did Barnabas need Paul?
6. See I Cor. 12:17-26. What gifts do you not have
that others in your church/small group do have?
7. What role did prophecy fulfill? What is the place
of prophecy today?
8. Is there a group that needs "relief" that is of
particular concern to you?

LIBERAL
The word of love and openness
(John 8:1-11)

1. Describe an early childhood experience of
shame. How did you react at the time?
2. What is the importance of Jesus sitting down to
teach?

3. The woman caught in adultery was brought to judgement. But where was the man caught in adultery? What might his absence tell Jesus about the assumptions of the Scribes and Pharisees?

4. What was the dilemma Jesus faced? Do you think it was a real dilemma for him?

5. Why did Jesus write in the sand?

6. Who left first and who left last? Why?

7. How were Jesus' words to the woman words of hope?

8. Will it be difficult for the woman not to sin again?

9. How liberal should the church be with "gross offenders?"

10. How has forgiveness functioned in your life as an impetus to change?

GLOBAL
The word of vision and vitality
(Mark 6:45-52)

1. In your experience of the church has there ever been a time in which you felt that, while there seemed to be growth on a number of fronts, the Lord himself seemed absent?

2. In the story that Mark gives us, what is Jesus doing for the young church as it confronts its difficulties? See Hebrews 7:25. How does that verse speak to their situation and yours?

3. In what ways is your church "making headway painfully?" Think of the worldwide (global) church. In what ways is it "making headway painfully?"

4. Are there ways in which the disciples' fear of Jesus in this story is mirrored in our contemporary western culture's fear of Jesus Christ? Even the church's fear of Jesus Christ? What might third world Christians have to teach us about this?

5. Mark says that the disciples "did not understand about the loaves." (v.52) What didn't they understand?

6. Why did Jesus mean to "pass by them" as he walked on the water?

7. What are some of the waves that threaten your local church today? The global church? And what can we do if our "hearts are hardened?"

ANGLICAN
A call to repentance and Comprehensiveness
(1 Pet. 2:4-10)

1. What family member functioned as a "cornerstone" in your home when you were growing up?

2. In the hour Peter envisions, who does the building? What role do the stones play?

3. What is "chosennes" intended to mean?

4. Who is the priesthood here? What does "priesthood" mean?

5 From the description of the cornerstone here, what positive and negative role does Peter see Christ playing in society?

6. Why would Peter's description of the church in v.9 be such a radical idea in the Roman culture of the day? In our day?

7. From what darkness have you been delivered?

8 Can you be part of the people of God without knowing that you have received mercy?

9. Do you see the "marks" of the comprehensive church here: evangelical, catholic, reformed, charismatic, liberal, global?

10. Which of the six descriptive words for the church in question 9 best/least describe your parish?

INDEX

Bruce, F.F., 143
Bruner, Frederick Dale,
Buddhism, 111
Bultmann, R., 128
Burdick, Donald W., 64
Butler, Samuel, 125

Calvin, John: Institutes, 81; and
    the real presence, 87; third use
    of the law, 82
Calvinism, 7, 84
Cambridge Camden Society, 63
Cambridge University, 19-2
    111-2, 161
Campus Crusade for Christ, 7
Camus, Albert, 152;
Canterbury Cathedral, 155;
Celtic Christianity, 45
Chadwick, Florence, 148
Chadwick, Henry, 54, 63
Charismatics: Cardinal Suenens on,
    107; and charisms, 96-7; in the
    church, 104-111; and experi-
    ence, 176; and spirituality,
    94, 165; and worship, 183
Christian Science, 111
Church: authority in, 130; body
    of Christ, 22; catholicity of,
    176; comprehensiveness of, 12,
    51,94, 107, 165, 168, 185;
    and culture,155, 161; discipline
    in, 35, 25; in, 105,174;
    government of, 51;
    inclusivity of, 177; need
    for continual reformation of,
    83; numerical growth in,
    124-5; persecuted, 159, 161;
    relation to Bible, 50;
    social concern and, 103,
    137, 165, 169; and the true
    church, 158; understood socio-
    logically, 22, 50, 100; unity of,
    54, 138; visibility and invisibility
    51-2, 177
Church Missionary Society. *See*
    Missionary concern

Church of England: and evangeli-
    cal awakening, 36, 170; in
    nineteenth century, 148; and
    patronage system, 21; and
    Puritans, 59-61,64; Reforma-
    tion of, 46- 7, 68-89; and un-
    educated clergy, 71
Church decline, 10
Clowney, Edmund, 63
Coats, William, 171
Collinson, Patrick, 64
Colson, Charles, 139
Columba, *See Celtic Christianity*
Confession, 58, 68, 74
Congregational Church, 156
Conservatism: attitudes of,
    123-4; and church growth,
    125; ethos of, 121-6; and the
    family, 123; and politics, 122;
    in Victorian era, 124-5
Controversy: doctrinal, 12, 158;
    ethical, 12; liturgical, 12, 88-9;
    on social issues and, 12, 97,
    140-1,
Coggan, Donald, archbishop of
    Canterbury, 110
Conscience,89, 140
"Consolatio", Archbishop
    Hermann's, 38
Conversion, 13,35, 103
Cranmer, Thomas: on the Book
    of Common Prayer, 67,86;
    on the church, 51; in prison,
    69; on the real presence, 87
Creeds, 13,45,49,53, 155
Cross, F.L., 90
Cults, 107
Culture: in age of uncertainty,
    100; and conservatism, 122;
    and revelation, 30; rootlessness
    of,9

Dulles, Avery, 137
Dunn, James, 107,115

Ebeling, G., 128
Ecclesiology, 12
Ecumenical movement, 16, 138

evangel, 30; focus on, 14; and the laity,105; modern movement 152; and the New Testament church, 104; and unity, 138

Modernism, 155

Modernity, 9, 16, 129, 131

Montreal Declaration, The, 164

Monasteries, 46, 70-2

Moody, D.L., 140

Moorman, J.R.H., 64, 90, 172

Moralism, 27

Morality, *See Ethics*

Moravians, 31

More, Hannah: Academy of, 168; and the Clapham Sect, 169; and education, 169; and missions, 170; and moral reformation, 147; and social activism, 147

Muggeridge, Malcolm, 164

Muslims, 132-3

Mysticism, 114

Neal, John Mason, 63

Neill, Stephen, 162

Newbigin, Lesslie, 63, 144

New birth, 76

Newman, John Henry, 79

Newton, John, 83, 169

Ninian. *See Celtic Christianity*

Nietzsche, Friedrich, 153

Nigeria, 156, 164, 168

Noll, Peggy, 172

Oden, Thomas, 129

O'Donovan, Oliver, 4

Old Testament, 27

Orthodoxy: bishops as keepers of, 54; holding fast to, 26, 173; tests of, 158; variety within, 52;

Orthodoxy, Eastern, 52

Owerri, Diocese of, 147, 168

Oxford Movement, 48

Packer, J.I., 127

Parientlicism, 155

Papacy: errors of, 49; infallibility of, 71; power of, 46; Renaissance, 70; wealth of, 70

Pascal, Blaise, 164

Patrick. *See Celtic Christianity*

Penance, 73

Pentecostal churches: and catholicity, 52; and charismatics, 99; and Episcopal Church, 7; extremism of, 95-6; growth of, 110, 148; origins of, 98; spirituality of, 108; theology of, 97, 113; worship in, 183

Pickering, W.S.F., 17

Pietism, 155

Politics, 24

Post-modernism, 150, 153, 154

Prayer: effective, 181; ecumenical, 135; extempore, 43; and healing, 56, 181; "name it and claim it", 109

Prayer Book Society, 7

Preaching: Anglican, 159; charismatic, 105; evangelical, 36; evangelistic, 30; expositional 21, 155; irrelevant, 14, 160; of Jesus as Lord, 102; lectures on, 119; "poor preachers", 72 with power, 104; Puritan, 64; Reformational, 47, 69; scriptural, 43

Predestination, 165

Presbyterian Church, 44, 156

Priesthood of all believers, 33,35, 167

Prophecy, 100, 126, 136, 158 165, 183

Protestant churches, 14,48-9

Purgatory, 71

Puritans, 59-61,64, 155-6

Quakers, 156

Racism, 123

Radical theology, 129-30

Rahner, Karl, 172

217

Real presence, 86-8, 158

Reason: and liberal theology, 127; and tradition, 60, 154; versus wisdom, 160

Recovery groups, 9

Reformation: Anglican, 84-9, 158; and balance, 60; Continental, 73, 80; continual, 83, 136; and doctrine, 176; errors of, 9; and Luther, 77; watchwords of, 80

Relativism, 129

Religious Tract Society, 170

Renewal movements, 24

Revivalism, 32-3, 140

Revivals, 162

Ridley, Nicholas, 69, 89

Roman Catholic Church: and Anglican orders, 135, 143; auricular confession, 58; and charismatics, 98, 121; converts to, 8, 164; and Council of Trent, 78; in England, 46; and Extreme Unction, 57; and justification, 78-9; in Latin America, 148; on scriptural interpretation, 59; theology of, 156; on transubstantiation, 88; and Vatican II, 52,79

Romanticism, 140

Ruether, Rosemary, 129~30

Rushing, Byron, 178

Ryle, J.C., 90

Sacraments: adoration of elements, 88; appeal of, 149; effect of, 155; Hooker on, 61; sacramental acts, 110; and transubstantiation, 73, 85-8; ordained by Christ, 53; visible words, 43

St. Francis of Assisi, 72

St. Ignatius, 49

St. Paul: conversion of, 140; in Corinth, 108; to the Galatians, 75-6, 182; to the Romans, 77, 182; on the Holy Spirit, 102-3; on justification, 79; liberal approach to, 127; on wisdom, 162

St. Peter, 184-5

Saints, merits of, 71, 74

Sanctification, 79-83, 163, 173

Sartre, Jean Paul, 152

Satan, 49

Scripture Union, 172

Seitz, Christopher, 170, 173

Sexual: morality, 168

Shepherding movement, 109

Sheppherd, David, 112

Shoemaker, Samuel, 114, 160

Simeon, Charles, 19-22, 36, 165

Sin: bondage of, 161; deeper dimensions of, 134; and heresy, 161; and sickness, 58, 181; struggle with, 108

Socialism, 129

Society for New Testament Studies, 128

S.P.C.K., 170

Speaking in tongues, 7, 96, 98-9, 108

Spiritual warfare, 82,97,109

Spiritualism, 111

Spirituality: the occult, 166; new age, 166; disciplines,166; holiness, 166

Spitler, Russell P.,115

Spong, John, 162, 171

Stark, Rodney, 38

Stephens-Hodge, L. E. N., 38

Stewardship, 23, 125

Stott, John R. W., 90, 157, 162

Strachey, Lytton, 124-5

Suenens, Leon J., 107

Swing, William, ?

Sykes, Stephen, 17, 171

Taize, Prior of, 106

Tasker, R.V.G., 64

Televangelists, 97

Templeton Award, 139

Thirty-Nine Articles: on the Bible, 50; on ceremonies, 136; confessional nature of, 155-6;

on Extreme Unction, 58; on
justification, 80-1
Third World: bishops, 161;
Thomas, Philip, 172
Toon, Peter, 63, 90
Tower of London, 89
Tradition: authority of, 151;
guided by God, 52; and rea-
son, 60; under scripture, 1,
154; value of, 153
Travers, Walter, 64
Trent, Council of, 78
Tyalke, Nicholas, 64

Unanimity principle, 109
Vatican II, 52, 79
Virgin Birth, 126
Virgin Mary, 158
Virginia Theological Seminary,
140

Watson, David: on "baptism of
the Holy Spirit", 114; conver-
sion, 111; ministry in York,
93, 112; struggle with cancer,
112; theology of, 113; world
impact of, 93
Webber, Robert, 7, 149
Wescott, B.F., 130
Wesley, John, 31, 35, 84, 162, 164
Westminster Confession, 156
Wetzel, Todd, 4
Wheaton College, 7
White, Roger J., 115, 149
Whitefield, George, 35-6, 162,
164
Wilberforce, William, 169
Willimon, William, 16
Wingate, Andrew, 163, 172
Wisdom, 161
Witness, 103-5, 167
Women's Ordination, 157
Word of God: focus on, 43;
knowledge of, 68; as personal
message, 34; receptivity to,
24,36; as rule of faith, 136;

and truth, 102, 129;
Worship: and action, 170; and
the Anglican Reformation,
84-9, 157; charismatic,
105,111; contemporary, 152;
corporate, 167; desire for, 10;
diversity of rites, 51; God-centered, 149; liturgical, 9, 16,
44,126,136, 142,159,175;
and the mass, 73; material
order in, 110; with the mind,
13; music in, 100, 136, 152;
New Testament contrasted
with Old, 28; nourishment by,
8; Puritans on, 60
Wright,, N.T., 171
Wycliffe, John, 72

Yancey, Philip, 37
Youth: Anglicanism and, 163-4;
appeal to, 16; Holy Spirit
and, 105; ministries to, 24

Zeigler, Leslie, 143